A Summary of
Town and Country Planning Law
and the Law of
Compulso
and Com

A Summary of Town and Country Planning Law and the Law of Compulsory Purchase and Compensation

A. J. LOMNICKI
Dr. Iur (Krakow), LL.M. (London)

Lecturer in Law
at the Polytechnic of
the South Bank
London

B. T. BATSFORD LTD
London

First published 1973
© A. J. Lomnicki 1973

ISBN 0 7134 0531 7

Computer composition in England by
Eyre & Spottiswoode Ltd at Grosvenor Press, Portsmouth
Printed by the Anchor Press Ltd
Tiptree, England
for the publishers
B. T. Batsford Ltd
4 Fitzhardinge Street
London W1H 0AH

CONTENTS

PREFACE

There are a number of excellent, detailed books dealing with the law of Town and Country Planning, Compulsory Purchase and Compensation and these are listed in the Bibliography on page 129. Here a somewhat different approach has been adopted, in offering a basic introduction to these subjects.

This book is designed to meet the needs of those students who are preparing for professional examinations, or reading for degrees in Estate Management, Planning and allied academic disciplines. It may also be of use as a quick reference book for those already in professional practice.

I should like to thank my colleagues at the Polytechnic of the South Bank, both lawyers and planners who advised me on many problems, especially Mr G. F. Bowden, M.A.(Oxon), and my daughter Miss E. Z. Lomnicka, B.A., LL.B.(Cantab), who read the manuscript and made numerous suggestions. I must, of course, take full responsibility for any shortcomings which this book may still contain.

I have endeavoured to state the law as it was on 31 December 1972, but brief accounts of the new General Development Order 1973 and the new Land Compensation Bill appears as appendices.

TABLE OF STATUTES

TABLE OF STATUTORY INSTRUMENTS

TABLE OF CASES

PART I

Town and Country Planning Law

Note: In this part all section references are references to the Town and Country Planning Act 1971 unless otherwise stated.

Chapter 1

HISTORICAL OUTLINE

For centuries until the Industrial Revolution the tasks of the Government were, generally speaking, limited to ensuring order within the realm and security against outside invaders.

It was only after the Industrial Revolution that the complexity of modern life compelled Government to accept responsibility for many other problems, including the welfare of its citizens, the conditions of their homes, their education, health and standard of living.

Within administrative law we can discern three categories of legislation dealing with the living conditions of the population. These are Public Health Acts which were developed first, followed by Housing Acts and Town and Country Planning Acts.

The Public Health and Housing Acts deal with individual houses which are insanitary or otherwise unfit for human habitation and with groups of unfit houses. They do not, however, consider the problem of the general environment of houses. The problem of houses built within the close vicinity of factories, or factories built in residential area were not tackled until 1909, when the 'Housing, Town Planning, etc., Act' was passed. It was a timid step towards town planning. It gave local authorities powers to make 'town planning schemes' in respect of suburban land, with the general object of securing 'proper sanitary conditions, amenity and convenience in connection with the laying out and use of the land and of any neighbouring lands'. Such planning schemes could regulate the number of buildings on a site and the space between them, and also could provide for control of the appearance of the buildings and the purpose for which they might be used. It was also obligatory for the scheme to define zones in which only some specific types of building use would be permitted. Although the schemes did not yet accept the idea that developments invariably require permission from the local authority, they could indicate the types of development which required the application to and the permission of the local authority.

Further Acts developed the idea of planning. The Act of 1932 enabled local authorities to prepare planning schemes for any land in England and Wales and not merely for suburban land as had previously been the case.

It was only in 1947, however, that, for the first time, a comprehensive scheme of town and country planning was enacted.

Planning became not only the right, but also the duty of the local planning authorities and the lay out of the Act was logical and comparatively simple. It may be represented by the following four principles:

First, the local planning authorities were entrusted with the duty of preparing development plans for their area.

Second, in order to ensure that the development plan would be adhered to, a further important principle was introduced, viz. that any development (as defined in the Act) required the permission of the local planning authority. There were, however, some clearly defined exceptions, which are outlined later.

Third, any unauthorised development might have been subject to enforcement procedure under the Act.

Fourth, there was a right of compensation in certain circumstances, if the owner's rights were infringed due to the exercise of planning control; in some cases the owner was entitled to compel the local planning authority to buy the land from him, if, due to planning restrictions, it was rendered incapable of reasonably beneficial use.

The 1947 Act also contains a number of provisions in respect of other matters connected with planning (e.g. the conferring upon local authorities the power of compulsory acquisition of land for undertaking development).

The 1947 Act was amended on several occasions[1] in subsequent years, until finally, in 1962, the main Act and subsequent amending Acts were repealed and consolidated in the Town and Country Planning Act 1962.

In 1967, 20 years after the 1947 Act was enacted, experience had shown that the Act required considerable overhauling. A White Paper, entitled 'Town and Country Planning',[2] published in June 1967 pointed out some deficiencies in the exisiting legislation and suggested changes. 'Three major defects have now appeared in the

4

present system. First, it has become overloaded and subject to delays and cumbersome procedures. Second, there has been inadequate participation by the individual citizen in the planning process and insufficient regard to his interest. Third, the planning system has been functioning better as a negative control, than as a positive stimulus to the creation of a good environment. . . ." 'We must recognise that planning is now operating in a very different context from that immediately after the war. When the 1947 Act was being prepared, planning was based on the belief that our population was likely to remain stable and there was little appreciation at that time of the likely growth of motor traffic — and still less of the impact that it would have on the structure of our towns and on the countryside. . . .' '. . . the plans drawn up must also be realistic in financial terms and the demand they make on the main capital expenditure programmes must be reasonable in amount and timing'. '. . . People must be able to participate fully in the planning process and their rights must be safeguarded'.

The White Paper's views were accepted by Parliament and the Town and Country Planning Act 1968 was passed, amending the 1962 Act in many respects.

Part II of the 1962 Act relating to the making, approval and coming into operation of development plans has been repealed and replaced by the Part I of the 1968 Act.

The enforcement of planning control has been strengthened.

Some decentralisation and simplification of procedure in granting planning permission and in appeals against decisions has been effected.

The Act also contained a variety of changes of considerable importance in planning law.

Part I of the 1968 Act, relating to the procedure for the making of development plans, is coming into operation in stages by being introduced in various parts of the country as soon as the Secretary of State for the Environment is satisfied that the local planning authority is properly prepared to work the new procedure, as this new procedure gives the local authorities much more scope. For this reason both types of development plans, 'old style' and 'new style', are at present in operation.

After the 1968 Act came into operation, the town and country planning law again became too complicated. For this reason a new consolidating Act 'Town and Country Planning Act 1971' was passed and came into operation (with some exceptions given in Section 294) on 1 April 1972.

The Act, containing 295 Sections and 26 Schedules is comprehensive, consolidating the 1962 and the 1968 Town and Country Planning Acts and a number of other Acts as far as they deal with planning, the most important being the London Government Act 1963, the Control of Office and Industrial Development Act 1965, the Industrial Development Act 1966, the Civic Amenities Act 1967 and other.

However, just seven days after passing the consolidating planning Act in 1971, Parliament started amending it and on 27 July 1972 the 'Town and Country Planning (Amendment) Act 1972' received the Royal assent.

The most important change is the considerable limitation of public participation in planning. Apparently, in the Government's opinion, the provisions of the 1968 Act went too far in this respect.

Further changes in respect of local planning authorities have been introduced by the Local Government Act 1972,[3] which will come into operation on 1 April 1974 with some minor exceptions indicated in Section 273 of that Act.

Chapter 2

PLANNING AUTHORITIES

Central Authority

In Central Government the Minister responsible for town and country planning is the Secretary of State for the Environment.[1]

The powers and duties of the Secretary of State are very large and may be considered under the following headings:[2]

(a) Issuing Statutory Instruments. The Town and Country Planning Act may be considered as a skeleton act, since many technical and other important details are left to the statutory instruments issued by the Secretary of State. Thus many orders supplement the provisions of the Act, and they will be mentioned in their proper place, but here it is appropriate to say that the General Development Order covers many aspects of planning law. For instance, many classes of development are permitted by the General Development Order without the necessity of applying for planning permission.[3]

(b) In some cases decisions of the local planning authority require approval by the Secretary of State. For instance 'old style' development plans and the 'new style' structure plans require approval by the Secretary of State for their validity.

(c) In many cases a person aggrieved by a decision of a local planning authority has a right of appeal to the Secretary of State. For instance there is a right of appeal against the refusal of planning permission, against the granting of it subject to conditions, or against an enforcement order, etc. Although such appeals should be directed to the Secretary of State, Schedule 9 allows a number of appeals to be decided by a person nominated by the Secretary of State, i.e. by an inspector. This aspect will be discussed later.

(d) In some cases the Secretary of State may give directions, either in general, or in particular matters. For example a direction may be given laying down the procedure to be followed where

the planning authority wishes to grant planning permission which
is not in accordance with the development plan. The Secretary of
State may also issue a direction 'calling in' an application for
planning permission in a particular case.

(e) If the Secretary of State considers that a local planning
authority has failed to fulfil some duty under the Town and
Country Planning Act, he may himself take action or entrust the
action to another local authority.

(f) Claims for compensation, when planning decisions restrict
new developments, which may be claimed under Part VII of the
1971 Act are dealt with by the Secretary of State.[4]

(g) Some decisions of the Secretary of State are of a judicial
nature, interpreting the existing law. Under Section 53 the
Secretary of State may, on appeal from the local planning
authority or at first instance, determine whether intended action
would constitute development and if so, whether planning permission is necessary.

In addition to these functions given by statute, the Secretary of
State shapes the policy of the local planning authorities by advice
and information, which is usually contained in circulars.

Local Planning Authorities

Under the Local Government Act 1972, which comes into force
on 1 April 1974, England outside Greater London will be divided
into six metropolitan counties and 39 non-metropolitan counties.
The metropolitan counties are Greater Manchester, Merseyside,
South Yorkshire, Tyne and Wear, West Midlands and West Yorkshire. The metropolitan and non-metropolitan counties will be
divided into some 369 districts.[5] Wales will be divided into nine
counties and 36 districts.[6]

The local planning authorities are the council of a county for the
county and the council of a district for the district.[7]

The Secretary of State may by order constitute a joint planning
board for an area of any two or more local planning authorities.
Thus they may be a joint planning board as a county planning
authority covering areas (or parts of the areas) of two or more
county councils, or as a district planning authority covering areas (or
parts of the areas) of two or more district councils. Such a joint
planning board may be created only after holding a local inquiry
unless all the councils concerned have consented to the making of
the order.

8

Schedule 1 to the 1971 Town and Country Planning Act contains detailed provisions in respect of the joint planning board. The members of the joint planning board will be appointed by the constituent councils and it shall be a body corporate, having its own legal personality. Joint planning boards have been constituted for the Lake District and for the Peak District.

A local planning authority may establish a planning committee and the committee may exercise any of the planning functions within delegated authority by the council except the power to borrow money or to levy precepts for rates. A planning committee may appoint subcommittees (Section 101 of the Local Government Act 1972).

Any two or more local planning authorities may concur in establishing a joint advisory committee for the purpose of advising these authorities as to the preparation of the structure and of the local plans, provided that at least two-thirds of the members shall be the members of one or other of these authorities. (Section 102 of the Local Government Act 1972).

Any of the local planning authorities' functions may be discharged by an officer of the authority, provided that arrangements to this effect are made by the local authority concerned and/or by the planning committee or subcommittee (Section 101(1)(a) of the Local Government Act 1972).

Until 31 March 1974 the local planning authorities are councils of counties or county boroughs. There are provisions for the delegation of some functions to councils of county districts and to officers of local authorities (Sections 1-4 of the Town and Country Planning Act 1971).

The Greater London area is organised differently for the purpose of carrying out the provisions of the town and country planning law, although the Local Government Act 1972 in many respects organised the local planning authorities in a way similar to that operating in Greater London. The special provisions existing for the Greater London area are described in outline in Chapter XVI.

County and District Planning Authorities. Their Respective Jurisdictions

The general principle stated by Section 182(1) of the Local Government Act 1972 is that all functions conferred on local planning authorities by or under the Town and Country Planning

Act 1971 shall be exercisable both by county and district planning authorities.

This general principle, however, is subject to numerous qualifications given in Schedule 16 to the Local Government Act 1972.

Schedule 16 divides the jurisdiction between the county and district planning authorities under the following headings:

(a) structure and local plans;
(b) planning and special control;
(c) compensation for planning restrictions;
(d) purchase notices.

The division of responsibility between the two tiers of local planning authorities will be discussed when each of the above aspects are dealt with.

There is one exception to the division arranged in Schedule 16: all functions in a national park conferred by or under the Town and Country Planning Act 1971 are within the jurisdiction of the county authority (Section 182(4) of the Local Government Act 1972).

Chapter 3

DEVELOPMENT PLANS. OLD AND NEW STYLE

Introduction

It was in 1947 that the local planning authorities were, for the first time, instructed to prepare development plans and the Town and Country Planning Act 1947 set out the detailed procedure under which the development plans should be made. This part of the 1947 Act was later consolidated in Part II of the 1962 Act, and now appears in Schedule 5 to the 1971 Act.

The new procedure, created by the 1968 Act, replaced the 'old style' development plans, but the 'new style' development plans apply only to those parts of the country which have been indicated by an order issued by the Secretary of State. Thus, for the time being, the country is still governed by the 'old style' development plans (Schedule 5 to the 1971 Act) except where 'new style' development plans have been introduced on the decision of the Secretary of State. The 'new style' development plans are now dealt with by Part II of the 1971 Act.

Both types of the plans therefore require consideration.

Old Style

Section 1 of Schedule 5 to the 1971 Act requires any local planning authority to submit to the Secretary of State for the Environment a development plan.

The plan should indicate:

(a) the manner in which the land covered by the plan is to be used;

(b) the stages, by which the development plan is to be carried out.

The plan consists of a basic map and a written statement (both obligatory), together with such other maps as may be appropriate. Examples of these special maps are a town map, an inset map, a comprehensive development area map, a street map or a programme map.

11

A development plan may:

(a) define the sites of the proposed roads, buildings, airfields, parks, pleasure grounds, nature reserves and other open spaces;

(b) allocate areas for agricultural, residential or industrial purposes. Under the 1962 Act it could also designate areas being subject to compulsory purchase, but the possibility of this designation has been repealed by the 1968 Act, which conferred upon local authorities a straightforward power to acquire land compulsorily without the necessity of designating it in the development plan.

A development plan is prepared by the local planning authority and must be approved by the Secretary of State.

A notice of submission of a plan for approval by the Secretary of State must be given in the *London Gazette* and in the local newspapers; the notice must indicate the place where the copies of the plan may be inspected. A Regulation issued by the Secretary of State[1]) prescribes detailed procedure regarding objections which may be made by any interested person and details of the procedure to be adopted in the preparation and approval of development plans. Persons objecting may send their objections to the Secretary of State within the time prescribed by the Regulation. The Secretary of State must either hold a local inquiry or give objectors a hearing before an Inspector. The Secretary of State may afterwards approve the development plan with or without modifications. Under Section 6(3) of the Schedule the Secretary of State is authorised to hold discussions with the local planning authority or any other authority or person without inviting objectors to be present. In this case the rule of natural justice '*audi alteram partem*', as expressed in the case of Errington v. Minister of Housing and Local Government,[2] is excluded.

Under Section 3 of Schedule 6 any person aggrieved by a development plan approved by the Secretary of State may make an application to the High Court within six weeks and the Court (apart from the power of issuing an interim order suspending the operation of the plan) may quash the plan if satisfied that the plan is 'ultra vires', or that the interests of the applicant have been substantially prejudiced by a failure to comply with any requirements of the Act or of any Regulations issued under the Act.

Apart from this right of making an application to the High Court a development plan cannot be questioned in any legal proceedings whatsover; this seems to indicate that the plan cannot even be questioned by the prerogative order of *certoriari*.

The development plan must be reviewed every five years, or more often if the local planning authority wishes or the Secretary of State so instructs. The procedure for amending the existing development plan is the same as for preparing the original plan.

The Secretary of State has a default power. If a local planning authority neglects any of its duties in connection with the preparation of the development plan, the Secretary of State may himself take the necessary action or authorise some other planning authority to act.

New Style

The 'new style' development plan is dealt with in Part II of the 1971 Town and Country Planning Act (Sections 6-21) as amended by the Town and Country Planning (Amendment) Act 1972 (Sections 1-4) and the Local Government Act 1972 (Sections 182-184 and Schedule 16).

As the new style plan entrusts to the local planning authorities a much wider power than the old style, it is only being introduced in those areas where the local authority is financially strong and has a solid and efficient planning organisation. It will be gradually extended, but so far Statutory Instruments have been issued arranging for the commencement of Part II of the Act in respect only of the following ten areas:

(a) Teesside and North Riding of Yorkshire;

(b) the county boroughs of Portsmouth and Southampton and specified parts of Hampshire;

(c) City of Leicester and Leicestershire;

(d) and (e) two selected areas in the West Midlands;

(f) Buckinghamshire;

(g) North Wales (Anglesey, Carnarvonshire, Denbighshire, Flintshire and Merioneth);

(h) South-East Wales (county boroughs of Cardiff, Merthyr Tydfil, Newport and Swansea and the counties of Glamorgan and Monmouthshire);

(i) Brighton and parts of East and West Sussex;

(j) county boroughs of Norwich, Great Yarmouth and Ipswich and counties of Norfolk and East Suffolk.[3]

The reasons for introducing the 'new style' development plans were stated in the White Paper as the advisability of simplifying the procedure, decentralisation and the giving of a greater share to the citizens in influencing the contents of the plan ('Town and Country Planning' June 1967 Cmnd 3333).

The development plans are prepared in two stages: structure plan and local plans. The Secretary of State is required to confirm the structure plan only; the local plans are prepared and approved by the local planning authority and sent to the Secretary of State solely for information purposes.

Under Section 6 the preparation of the structure plan is the responsibility of the county council and they are to institute the surveys, on which the structure plan will be based, as it is recognised that some reliable research is necessary before the structure plan is made. The survey does not necessarily have to be conducted by the authority itself, it may be entrusted to outside consultants.

The survey, once completed, must be kept under constant review, and the local planning authority may at any time institute a fresh survey and shall do so, if directed by the Secretary of State.

The matters to be examined in the survey shall include the following points:

(a) the principal physical and economic characteristics of the area of the authority (including the principal purposes for which land is used) and, so far as they may be expected to affect that area, of any neighbouring areas;

(b) the size, composition and distribution of the population of that area (whether resident or otherwise);

(c) the communications, transport and traffic of that area, and, if advisable, of any neighbouring areas;

(d) any consideration which may be expected to affect any matters mentioned above;

(e) any other matters prescribed by the Secretary of State;

(f) any changes projected and the effect of these changes.

Thus, in essence, the survey covers land, population and population movements.

There is also a duty of the local planning authority to consult, if necessary, any other authority about those matters insofar as it may be affected.

The local planning authorities shall prepare and send to the Secretary of State a report of their survey and submit to him for his approval a structure plan for their area (Section 7).

The structure plan, which must be a written statement (it should be noted that it may not be a map), will:

(a) formulate the local planning authority's policy and general proposals in respect of the development and other use of land in that area (including measures for the improvement of the physical environment and the management of traffic);

(b) state the relationship of those proposals to general proposals for the development and other use of land in neighbouring areas; and

(c) contain such matters as may be prescribed by the Secretary of State.

The structure plan must be justified by the results of the survey and shall have regard to:

(a) the current policies of the region as a whole;

(b) the resources available;

(c) other matters as directed by the Secretary of State.

The structure plan must indicate 'action areas', i.e. areas selected for early development. The Government spokesman during the debate about the Act in the House of Commons indicated that areas should be treated as 'action areas' if development is intended to be carried out within ten years and this has been confirmed by the Regulations (Town and Country Planning. Structure and Local Development Plans Regulations 1971 S.I.1109).

A structure plan also contains diagrams, illustrations and descriptive matter, and this is the main difference between the old and the new style development plans. The old development plan was a map with explanation; the new one is a written statement without any map, but with diagrams illustrations and descriptive matter. The latter is a general statement of policy and does not show how any particular piece of land is affected. For this reason it was hoped that there would not be many objections by individual owners, but rather that problems of general policy only would be discussed during the procedure prescribed for the approval of the structure plan.

Whilst preparing a structure plan, the local planning authority must give adequate publicity to this fact, and provide an opportunity to all persons to make representations, if they wish. When the structure plan has been prepared and submitted to the Secretary of State for approval, again publicity should be given to this and all persons should be made aware that they can make objections to the Secretary of State (Section 8).

This is another important difference between the old and the new style. The public at large is entitled to take part in preparing the plan by making *representations* and, in addition, can make *objections* against the draft of the prepared plan. In the old style only objections were allowed.

The local planning authority, when submitting the plan to the Secretary of State, must show what steps have been taken to comply with the requirements regarding publicity, etc, and that the authority has given consideration to the views of the persons who have made representations.

If the Secretary of State is not satisfied that the local planning authority has acted properly in preparing the plan, he should return the plan for defects to be remedied. (Section 9.)

The Secretary of State may either approve the plan with, or without modifications, or reject it. If the plan is rejected by the Secretary of State, objections do not require to be considered. Otherwise, the Secretary of State has to consider any objections. Under the 1971 Act he had either to afford objectors an opportunity to be heard by an Inspector, or to arrange for a local inquiry to be held. In either case the local planning authority was entitled to be represented. But this procedure created a problem. The Greater London Development Plan inquiry had to look into some 21,000 objections and, of course, the expense and delay was enormous. The Government came to the conclusion that the issues treated by the Greater London Plan (and other structure plans) are mostly 'strategic' ones of little interest to the individual property owner, and that he will be able to defend his rights by objections to the local plans at a later stage. Therefore a new procedure has been introduced by Section 3 of the Town and Country Planning (Amendment) Act 1972 which applies only to structure plans and to those local plans which, exceptionally, have to be approved by the Secretary of State.

Under the new procedure, introduced by the 1972 Act, anyone can submit a written objection and the Secretary of State must consider all such submissions. He will then select the broad strategic and key issues, according to his discretion, which issues will be referred to a person or persons for examination in public. Neither the objectors nor the local planning authority will have the right to appear at the examination unless invited by the Secretary of State to do so, although the panel holding the examination will have power to invite additional persons. The examination under these provisions will be under the supervision of the Council on Tribunals, but in other aspects will not be considered to be a public inquiry.

Thus, these provisions considerably limit the role of the citizens in planning advocated so eloquently by the White Paper in 1967.

Before eventually approving the structure plan, the Secretary of State, in a similar way as in the 'old style', may consult with any local planning authority or other persons.

At any time after the approval of a structure plan, the local planning authority may submit to the Secretary of State an alteration to the structure plan. They have to take this action if so directed by the Secretary of State (Section 10).

It may happen that two or more local planning authorities responsible for the preparation of a structure plan come to the conclusion that it would be advisable to prepare a joint survey, report on a survey, and to prepare a structure plan covering two or more areas of the local planning authorities. For this reason Section 10A (introduced by the Town and Country Planning (Amendment) Act 1972) states that any two or more local planning authorities may apply to the Secretary of State for his consent to their areas or any part thereof being treated for the purposes of the preparation of a structure or local development plan as a combined area and, if the Secretary of State agrees, the local authorities concerned may institute a joint survey, submit a joint report on the survey and jointly prepare and submit to the Secretary of State a structure plan for the combined area.

Section 10B introduced by the Town and Country Planning (Amendment) Act 1972 allows the local planning authority to withdraw the structure plan submitted to the Secretary of State for approval before it is approved.

Development Plan Schemes

This is a new concept created by the Local Government Act 1972 (Section 183 of the Local Government Act 1972 inserting Section 10C into the Town and Country Planning Act 1971). The county planning authority in consultation with the district planning authorities of each county shall make, and afterwards keep under review (and amend it if they think fit) a 'development plan scheme' for the preparation of local plans for those areas in the county which are to be covered by the local plans (with the exception of any part in the county which is included in a National Park).

The development plan scheme:

(a) designates the authority responsible for the preparation of each local plan for the area in question, specifying the title and nature of each local plan for the area and giving an indication of its scope;

(b) sets out a programme for the preparation of the several plans for that area;

(c) indicates the relationship between the several local plans for that area.

A copy of the scheme should be sent to the Secretary of State for information.

The Secretary of State has wide powers in respect of the development plan schemes, as he may direct a county planning authority to prepare a development plan scheme before a date specified in the direction and, if necessary, to amend the existing scheme. If a district planning authority is dissatisfied with the proposals of the county planning authority for a development plan scheme, or if the county planning authority fails to amend the scheme according to the instruction issued by the Secretary of State, the Secretary of State may himself make or amend the scheme.

Local Plans

The general rule is that local plans are the responsibility of district councils.

There are, however, two exceptions to this rule:

(a) in respect of an area in a National Park (Section 2A of the Town and Country Planning Act 1971 as enacted by Section 182 of the Local Government Act 1972);

(b) the structure plan for an area may provide that local plans (if provisions to the contrary are not made in the development plan scheme) will be prepared exclusively by the county planning authority (Section 10C(5) of the Town and Country Planning Act 1971 as enacted by Section 183(2) of the Local Government Act 1972).

The local planning authority, on whom falls the responsibility for the preparation of a local plan, may prepare such a plan when the structure plan is in the course of preparation, or is submitted to the Secretary of State for approval.

When the structure plan has been approved, the local planning authority must, as soon as practicable, consider the desirability of preparing, and if appropriate prepare one or more local plans (Section 11(1) and (2) of the Town and Country Planning Act 1971 as amended by Paragraph 1 of the 16th Schedule to the Local Government Act 1972).

A local plan consists of a map and a written statement and shall:

(a) formulate proposals for the development and other use of land;

(b) contain such matters as may be prescribed by the Secretary of State.

A local plan contains such diagrams, illustrations and descriptive matter as appropriate. If there is an action area indicated in the structure plan, a local plan for that area is obligatory. The local plan must confirm generally to the structure plan. Different local plans may be prepared for different purposes for the same part of the area covered by the structure plan. Thus local plans are either plans with varying degrees of detail about a particular part of the area, or plans whose purpose concerns some particular aspect of planning for a rather wider area. There may be action area plans, or district plans covering larger parts of the area of the local planning authority, and even much smaller local plans dealing with a particular problem of some area within the district.

The primary purpose of a local plan, other than an action area plan, is to guide the authority and developers in respect of possible development of the land covered by the plan. The system is designed to be of the utmost flexibility and the amount of detail which goes into any particular local plan will depend on the nature of the proposals it contains.

A local planning authority, who proposes the preparation of a local plan, shall give adequate publicity to this fact and allow the persons interested an opportunity to make representations which have to be considered by the local planning authority when the draft plan is being prepared (Section 12). When the draft of the local plan is ready the local planning authority shall make copies of the draft plan available for inspection and send a copy to the Secretary of State. Time must be given to the objectors to raise objections to the draft of the plan. The Secretary of State may direct the local planning authority to comply with procedural requirements if he thinks that they have not been adhered to.

The local planning authority must consider objections that have been raised and must either hold a local enquiry, or

19

arrange a private hearing before a person appointed by the Secretary of State (Section 13).

After considering the objections and the report of the Inspector who held the local inquiry or hearing, the local planning authority may by resolution adopt the plan. The Secretary of State does not, as a general rule, approve the local plan (it is sent to him for information only), but has a right to direct that a particular plan shall not take effect unless approved by him (Section 14).

A local plan may be amended at any time after complying with the procedure prescribed for the preparation of the original plan (Section 15).

If a local planning authority is in default in preparing any survey, structure plan or local plan, which is obligatory (e.g. action area plan), the Secretary of State may either take action himself, or entrust the action to another local planning authority (Section 17).

The Secretary of State has issued a Statutory Instrument with respect to the form and contents of structure and local plans and with respect to the detailed procedure to be adopted in preparation of the plan (The Town and Country Planning (Structure and Local Plans) Regulations 1972 — Cmnd 1154).

Chapter 4

DEFINITION OF DEVELOPMENT

Sections 22-24 define development and set out the general principle that planning permission is required for the effecting of any development of land.

Development means the carrying out of building, engineering, mining or other operations in, on, over or under land, or the making of any material change in the use of any building or other land (Section 22).

'Building operations' (Section 290) include rebuilding operations, structural alterations of or any addition to the buildings and other operations normally undertaken by a person carrying on business as a builder. 'Engineering operations' include the formation or laying out of means of access to highways. The words 'mining operations' are not defined in the Act, but 'minerals' includes all minerals and substances in or under land of a kind ordinarily worked for removal by undergrounds or surface working, except that it does not include peat cut out for purposes other than for sale. 'Other operations' should be taken, under the *eiusdem generis*, rule of construction as some acts which change the physical characteristic of the land, or what is under it or in the air above it (Cheshire C.C. v. Woodward 1962 1 All .E.R. 517). In this case the Minister, on an enforcement notice appeal, held that the placing on the land of a coal bagging hopper on wheels resting on concrete blocks and a mobile conveyor also on wheels, both in a coal yard, was not development (although the Inspector reported that although both structures were on wheels, it would be difficult to move them and that such movements were unlikely whilst they were in use). The Divisional Court held that the Minister had not erred in law. This case illustrates that the operation must create a permanent situation and that the operation must annex the building (or structure) to the land. For this reason the placing of caravans on land is not an operation, but a way of using the land (this means it is a development, but under the second part

21

of Section 22 'material change in the use of any building or other land').

It is not easy to illustrate by examples what is meant by 'other operations', but no doubt removal of topsoil, so far, as it is not included in 'engineering or mining operation' would be considered 'other operation'. Whether the demolition of a building is an operation constituting development is an open question. Until recently it was assumed that the demolition of a building is not a development (e.g. Howell v. Sunbury-on-Thames U.D.C. 1963), but in a recent case (Coleshill and District Investment Co Ltd v. Minister of Housing and Local Government 1969 2 All E.R. 525) the House of Lords refused to say that the demolition was not development and left the issue open, although Lord Upjohn's dicta indicated that, in his opinion, demolition may be development: 'there is nothing in Section 12 (now Section 22 of the 1971 Act) which makes it plain that demolition per se or simpliciter is necessarily excluded from the very wide words of Section 12(1) (now Section 22(1))'.

The second type of development is 'the material change in the use of a building or other land'. This definition creates considerable difficulties of interpretation, because it is a matter of degree whether the change in question is 'material' or not. It seems that the general test is, whether the change in the use will completely alter the character of the land or building or not. Sometimes the question will depend on the degree of change. Thus in the case Guildford R.D.C. v. Penny (1959 2 All E.R. 111) an increase in the number of caravans from 8 to 27 was accepted by the Queen's Bench Division as concerning a matter of fact and not law and as such was not subject to revision by the High Court on appeal from the Magistrates' Court on a case stated. The Magistrates did not consider it material change in the use of the land. But in another case Lord Denning said that an increase from 24 to 78 caravans might well amount to a material change of use (Esdell Caravan Parks Ltd v. Hemel Hempstead R.D.C. 1966, 3 WLR 1238). Moreover in yet another case (Birmingham Corporation v. Minister of Housing and Local Government and Habib Ullah 1963, 3.W.L.R. 937) the owner of two houses which had been in single family occupation installed several families in each. The Minister considered that there had been no material change of use as the houses remained residential. On appeal by the local planning authority the court held that the Minister had erred in law saying that there could not be a material change in the use if the house has remained residential. Thus it is a matter of fact and degree in each case.

The general definition of development as stated in Section 22 — which is simple enough — is subject to some qualifications, and this makes the meaning of development, and particularly those developments which require permission, rather a complex one.

The definition is qualified in the following respects:

(a) Subsections 3 and 4 of Section 22 declare 'for the avoidance of doubt' that the three changes in the use of land, specified in these Subsections are development;

(b) Subsection 2 of Section 22 enumerates three operations and three changes in the use of the land which are not considered to be a development within the meaning of the Act;

(c) Section 23 enumerates six changes of use which are development, but do not require planning permission;

(f) permission for some developments is granted by the General Development Order issued by the Secretary of State under Section 24, and as such those developments do not require individual planning permissions.

Each of these qualifications will be discussed separately.

The following three changes in the use of the land are declared to involve a material change in the use of land and as such require planning permission:

(a) the use as two or more separate dwelling-houses of any building previously used as a single dwelling-house. In simple terms the conversion of a single dwelling-house into flats requires planning permission, although there is a general rule that works which do not affect external appearance of the building are not developments;

(b) the deposit of refuse or waste material on land notwithstanding that the land is already used for that purpose, if either the superficial area of the deposit is thereby extended, or the height of the deposit is thereby extended and exceeds the level of the land adjoining the site.

(c) the use of land for the display of advertisement on any external part of a building shall be treated as involving a material change of use. (It must be noted, however, that some advertisements are permitted under the 'Town and Country Planning (Control of Advertisements) Regulations 1969' — S.I.1532).

Thus planning authorities are given control over the display of advertisements as the amenities of the area may be affected by undesirable advertisements.

The following three operations and three changes in the use of the land shall not be taken for the purpose of the Act to involve development of the land:

(a) the carrying out of the works for the maintenance, improvement or alteration of any building being works which affect only the interior of the building, or which do not materially affect the external appearance of the building and are not works for making good war damage. But it has been held that the restoration to the same design of a building of which only the original foundation, damp course and two walls remained, was a reconstruction constituting development and not only maintenance of repair.[1] Also the replacement of a hedge by a fence is not maintenance, but development.[2] If works begun after 5 December 1968 they must not alter the building by providing additional space below the ground (This last amendment was introduced by the 1968 Act and for this reason applies only to the alterations started after 5 December 1968).

The provisions of this subsection require some explanation. Any work which does not affect the external appearance of the buiding does not concern the planning authority, as such work does not affect the environment of the land in question. But three exceptions should be noted: the conversion of a house into separate flats requires permission, because from the point of view of planning (density of population, traffic, etc) such a change is material; secondly, the planning authority require full control over making good war damage, as it may be in the interests of planning that the house should not be repaired or re-built to its pre-war style, but that the war damage should create an opportunity to develop the land according to modern ideas; thirdly it is undesirable to allow the extension of a building underground without supervision, as this may weaken its foundations or the space may be required by the statutory undertakers.

(b) the carrying out by a local authority of any works required for the maintenance or improvement of a road, being works carried out on land within the boundaries of the road. Thus those works include any improvement of the road, but not its widening.

(c) the carrying out by a local authority or statutory undertakers of any works for the purpose of inspecting, repairing or renewings

24

of any sewers, mains, pipes, cables or other apparatus, including the breaking open of any street or other land for that purpose;

(d) the use of any building or other land within the curtilage of a dwelling house for any purpose incidental to the enjoyment of the dwelling house as such (it should be noted that the provision applies only to a change in the use and not to operations, i.e. does not include erection of any additional structure);

(e) the use of any land for the purposes of agriculture or forestry and the use, for any of those purposes, of any building occupied on land so used. As the use of any land (or building) has to be for agriculture or forestry, it does not include the changing of use from agricultural storage to a farm labourer's cottage. Such a change is development.[3] 'Agriculture' is very widely defined in Section 290, but it does not include horse breeding for show jumping, as these animals are not used in farming.[4] An egg-vending machine placed by a roadside on a poultry farm was considered a material change of use.[5]

(f) In the case of buildings or other land which are used for a purpose of any class specified in any order made by the Secretary of State under this Section, the use thereof for any other purpose of the same class. This means that any change of use within the same class specified by the Order (Town and Country Planning (Use Classes) Order 1972 No 1385 which revoked and re-enacted with amendments 1963 Order No 708), is allowed, even if it is material change.

In order to understand the provisions of this Order, which is discussed presently, it is necessary to become acquainted with some definitions introduced by it:

(a) an 'industrial building' is defined as a building (other than a building in or adjacent to and belonging to a quarry or mine and other than a shop), used for the carrying on of any process for, or incidental to any of the following purposes, namely:

— the making of any article, or part of any article, or

— the altering, repairing, ornamenting, finishing, cleaning, washing, packing or canning, or adapting for sale, or breaking up for demolition of any article, or

— without prejudice to the foregoing paragraphs, the getting, dressing or treatment of minerals.

Industrial buildings are divided into three classes: light industrial building, general industrial building and special industrial building. A light industrial building is one in which the processes carried out or the machinery installed are such as could be carried on or installed in any residential area without detriment to the amenity of that area by reason of noise, vibration, smell, fumes, smoke, soot, ash, dust, or grit. A special industrial building means one used for the purposes specified in Classes V-IX. Buildings in these classes include those whose use can be classified as 'offensive trades' under the Public Health Act 1936. A general industrial building is any industrial building which is neither light nor special.

(b) the word 'office' is defined as to include a bank, but not post office or a betting office;

(c) the word 'shop' means a building used for the carrying on of any retail business wherein the primary purpose is selling of goods by retail. The following among others are shops: a hairdresser, an undertaker, ticket agency, a receiving office for goods to be cleaned, washed, or repaired and a building used for other purposes appropriate to a shopping area. The definition does not include a building used for a funfair, garage, petrol filling station, office, hotel or premises licensed for the sale of intoxicating liquors for consumption on the premises, betting shops and, since 1972 launderettes, cafés and restaurants.

The order permits change within the same class (and there are 18 of them). It should be noted, however, that a change from one class to another is allowed if the change is not material, as only a material change constitutes development.

Of the 18 classes only the first four are of general application.

Class I

A change of use from one to another type of shop; but planning permission is required for a change into the following shops: hot food shop, a tripe shop, a shop for sale of pet animals or birds, a cat's meat shop or a shop for the sale of motor vehicles.

Class II

A change from one type of office into another.

Class III

A change of use of a light industrial building into another light industrial building.

Class IV

A change of use of general industrial building into another general industrial building.

26

Other use classes are less important. For example a hospital may become an institution for old people, or a mental hospital may become a home for epileptics; an exhibition hall may become a concert hall, a theatre may become a cinema, etc.

Even a change within a class requires permission if the local planning authority, on granting planning permission adds a condition that only a specified use is allowed. If the intended change within the class would involve a breach of the condition imposed, the developer must apply for planning permission.

A further qualification of the definition of development requiring planning permission is contained in Section 23, which states that the following matters are development, but do not require planning permission:

(a) the resumption (before 5 December 1968) of the normal use of land which, on 1 July 1948 was temporarily used differently;

(b) the use for an occasional purpose of land which, on 1 July 1948 was used for one purpose, but also for that another purpose (but one such resumption must have taken place before the beginning of 1969);

(c) when the land was unoccupied on 1 July 1948 but had before that date been occupied at some time on or after 7 January 1937, planning permission is not necessary in respect of any use of the land begun before 6 December 1968 for the purpose for which the land was last used before the appointed day (i.e. 1 July 1948).

These three provisions preserve the rights of persons, who were 'caught' by the provisions of the 1947 Act which, for the first time, introduced the requirements of obtaining planning permission. Their importance, of course, is gradually diminishing with the course of time.

(d) if planning permission is granted for a limited period, the resumption of use of the land as was previously used;

(e) where by a development order planning permission has been granted subject to limitations, permission is not required for the normal use of that land apart from the use in accordance with that permission, provided that such normal use does not contravene the provisions of the Act.

(f) if an enforcement notice has been served in respect of the unauthorised use of land, planning permission is not required for the resumption of the previous use.

27

The last qualification of the definition of development requiring planning permission arises from Section 24, which instructs the Secretary of State to issue a 'development order', which will provide for the granting of planning permission.

The General Development Order:[6]

— itself grants planning permission for developments specified in the Order;

— provides for the local planning authority to grant permission on an application by a person interested.

Thus the general principle is that a person seeking permission for development should apply to the local planning authority for such permission, unless the General Development Order grants such permission generally for some classes of development.

The classes of 'permitted development' issued by the General Development Order are important, as they permit many types of development of a minor nature without the need for applying for permission.

The planning permission granted for permitted development under the General Development Order is given subject to one, or other, or sometimes both of the following standard conditions:

— that the permission shall not authorise any development which involves the formation, laying out or material widening of a means of access to a trunk or classified road;

— that no development shall be carried out, which creates an obstruction to the view of persons using any highway used by vehicular traffic at or near any bend, corner, junction or inter-section so as to be likely to cause danger to such person.

Of the 23 classes of permitted development by the General Development Order, only classes I-XI are of general interest and importance; the remainder concern development by public bodies such as local authorities, the National Coal Board, etc.

The more important classes are given below (with regard to others, the General Development Order should be consulted).

Class I

Development within the curtilage of a dwelling house

This class permits the enlargement, improvement or other alter-ation of a dwelling house, so long as its cubic content (as ascertained by external measurement) is not increased by more than 1,750 cubic feet, or one tenth, whichever is greater, subject to a maximum 4,000 cubic feet. This permission is subject to the standard conditions 1 and 2 and to two other conditions: first, that the height of the building must not exceed the height of the original dwelling house; second, that no part of the building must project beyond the forwardmost part of the original dwelling house.

This class also contains the erection within the curtilage of a dwelling house of any building or enclosure (other than a dwelling, garage, stable, loose box or coach house) required for a purpose incidental to the enjoyment of the dwelling house as such.

This permission is subject to the standard conditions 1 and 2 and also to the further condition that the height must not exceed in the case of a building with a ridge roof 12 feet, or in any other case 10 feet.

Class II
Minor operations
This class authorises the erection of gates, fences, walls and other means of enclosure, provided that they do not exceed 4 feet in height when abutting on a road used by vehicles, or 7 feet in height in any other case.

Under this class the external painting of a building is also authorised, provided that it is not in the nature of advertisement.

Class III
Changes of use
This class authorises a change of use of a building from a general industrial building to a light industrial building (although it is a change from one class of uses to another, it is beneficial from the point of view of planning). It also permits the change of use of a restaurant to any type of shop (except a fried fish shop, a tripe shop, a shop for the sale of pet animals or birds, a cat's meat shop, or a shop for the sale of motor vehicles) and also a change of use to any type of shop from the five categories of shop mentioned above into a shop.

Class IV
Temporary buildings and uses
Under this head permission is given for the erection or construction on land of buildings, plant and machinery needed

temporarily in connection with the carrying of authorised development.

It also gives permission for the temporary use of land for any purpose on not more than 28 days in any calendar year, and permits the erection and placing of movable structure on the land for the purposes of that use. This permission is applicable to fairs, markets and camping.

Class V

Under this heading land not within the curtilage of a dwelling house may be used for recreation and instruction involving the use of tents (but not caravans) by members of a recreational organisation, which holds a certificate of exemption under Section 269 of the Public Health Act 1936 (such as the Boy Scouts Association).

Class VI

This class authorises the carrying out on agricultural land of more than one acre and comprised in an agricultural unit of all the building and engineering operations likely to be undertaken on a normal farm. The provision and alteration of dwellings, however, are not included. Some conditions are attached regarding the size and height of the buildings particularly in the vicinity of aerodromes.

Class VII
Forestry buildings and works
Similar permission is given in respect of building and other operations required for forestry.

Class VIII
Industrial development
Permission if given for additions to industrial buildings (by extension or new erections), but not beyond one-tenth of the cubic capacity of the original building. Permission is also given for various works and installations on industrial premises.

Class IX
Repairs to unadopted streets and private ways

Class X
Repairs to services
Under this class repairs of sewers, underground telephones, etc are allowed.

Class XI
War damaged buildings, works and plants
Although the replacement of war-damaged buildings is authorised under this class, the Secretary of State, who is entitled to exclude or limit some classes, excluded this class in many areas wishing to keep under control the re-building of towns after the destruction caused by the war. A similar power of exclusion is given to local authorities with the approval of the Secretary of State.

It will appear from the above discussion that the definition of development requiring planning permission is a complex one and problems may often arise, whether any intended work (be it an operation or change in the use of land) constitutes a development requiring permission.

For this reason Section 53 provides that if any person, who proposes to carry out any operation on land or to make any change of use in the land, wishes to have it determined beforehand whether the carrying out of this would constitute or involve development of land, or whether planning permission is required, he may apply to the local planning authority asking for the determination of that question.

There is a right of appeal to the Secretary of State against the determination of the local authority and a further right of appeal to the High Court on limited ground discussed later.

But it should be realised that any informal determinations are of limited value. Thus in one case[7] the borough engineer, in reply to an inquiry by a company wrote: '. . . the land has an existing user right as a builder's yard and no planning permission is, therefore, necessary'. The company bought the land and were subsequently served with an enforcement notice requiring them to stop using the land as a builder's yard. The Divisional Court held that, as a public authority could not fetter themselves by estoppel in the exercise of their statutory discretion to serve an enforcement notice, and so allowed the corporation's appeal against the quashing of the notice by the local magistrates under the enforcement procedure then in force. The position would be different if the local authority's certificate were issued under the procedure of Section 53. Thus informal applications and informal replies are of no legal validity.

Chapter 5

GENERAL PLANNING CONTROL

Applications for planning permission
Planning permission is required for the carrying out of any development on land, unless permission is granted in general terms by the Act itself or by the General Development Order (Sections 25-28).

The General Development Order 1963, as amended on the last occasion in 1969, prescribes the method of application and the procedure in dealing with the application.

The application is to be made on a form issued by the local planning authority and must include such particulars as the application form requires and must be accompanied by a plan sufficient to identify the land together with such other plans and drawings as are necessary to describe the development. The local planning authority may require such further information as is requisite to enable them to determine the application.

The developer, either before buying the land, or before incurring expense involved in the preparation of detailed plans, may apply for 'outline planning permission' which can be granted subject to any 'reserved matters' in respect of siting, design and external appearance of the building. The local planning is then committed to granting planning permission in some form or another and the planning permission is required only in respect of 'reserved matters'. If planning permission has been granted on an outline application subject to reserved matters of siting and design, the local planning authority may not, at a later stage, refuse planning permission for reasons outside the reserved matters (Hamilton v. West Sussex County Council 1958 9 P & C.R.299). The outline planning permission can be asked for only if the intended development includes the erection of a building and does not refer exclusively to a change of use.

The applicant for planning permission need not have a legal interest in the land in question. The application may be made by a prospective purchaser or lessee. Formerly the application could be made even without the knowledge of the owner of the land, but now the applicant has to submit one of the following four certificates (Section 27):

Certificate 'A'

This certificate states that the applicant is the estate owner or the lessee of the land in question. In this situation he is not required to notify anybody about the application.

Certificate 'B'

This certificate states that the applicant has given notice to all persons who, within the preceding 21 days, had been owners of the land and gives their addresses and names.

Certificate 'C'

This certificate is submitted if some of the persons entitled to the notice cannot be found.

Certificate 'D'

This certificate states that none of the owners can be found.

In the last two cases a notice must be published in a newspaper.

In addition, another certificate must be submitted, stating either that none of the land constitutes an agricultural holding, or that a notice has been given to all tenants of agricultural holdings.

The above notice must be accurate, since a false notice may involve criminal proceedings with a penalty of up to £100.

There are special provisions in Section 28 for additional publicity of any applications for a development affecting conservation areas.

Section 26 and the General Development Order prescribed that in five classes of development, being 'bad neighbours developments' a publication of the application in a local newspaper is necessary. These five classes of development are:

— the construction of buildings for use as a public convenience;

— the construction of buildings or other operations, or use of land for the disposal of refuse or waste materials;

— the construction of buildings or other operations or use of land for the purpose of sewage disposal;

— the construction of buildings or use of land for the purposes of a slaughter-house or knacker's yard;

— the construction of buildings and use of buildings for any of the following purposes, namely as a theatre, a cinema, a music hall, a dance hall, a skating rink, a swimming pool or gymnasium (not forming part of a school, college, or university), a Turkish or

34

other vapour or foam bath, or a building for indoor games.

If any person makes a representation concerning any of the above classes of development, the local planning authority must consider the representation.

In addition, the applicant in respect of 'bad neighbour developments' must post a notice on the land involved, stating that an application for planning permission is to be made. Such a notice must be left for not less than seven days and must be displayed in such a manner as to be easily visible and legible by members of the public, but the applicant is not responsible if the notice is removed or obscured by third persons.

Determination by the Local Planning Authority of Application for Planning Permissions. (Sections 29-35).

Upon the receipt of an application for planning permission the local planning authority must send a receipt to the applicant. The decision should be given to the applicant within two months, or within three months if the application affects a trunk road. Only by written consent of the applicant may these periods be exceeded. If the applicant does not receive the decision within the above periods, he is entitled to appeal to the Secretary of State as if his application had been refused.

In dealing with an application the local planning authority must have regard to the development plan, but may grant permission which does not agree with the development plan within authority given generally or specifically by the Secretary of State.

The local planning authority after having considered the application may:

— grant permission unconditionally;
— grant permission subject to such conditions as they think fit;
— refuse permission.

The decision must, of course, be in writing.

As the decision of the local planning authority is a vital document, defining the rights of the developer, it is important, that the decision should be clear and free from any ambiguity. If a problem of interpretation arises, it has been indicated by the Court of Appeal (Slough Estate Ltd v. Slough Borough Council and another, 1969 2 WLR (CA), 1970 2 WLR 1187 (HL)) that the grant of permission is the document issued by the authority and not the authority's resolution. On the other hand the House of Lords in the same case stated that 'since the purported planning permission was not complete or self-contained on the face of it in that inter alia it incorporated by referencce the plan submitted, it was proper to examine the correspondence leading up to the grant of planning permission with a view to ascertaining what the terms of the application were and how the plan was submitted and what functions it was intended to perform'.

Without prejudice to the general power given to the local authority to impose on planning permission such conditions as they think fit, the authority is empowered by Section 30(1) to impose conditions:

(a) regulating the development or use of any land under the control of the applicant (whether or not it is land in respect of which the application was made), or requiring the carrying out of works on any such land, insofar as it appears to the local planning authority to be expedient for the purposes or in connection with the development authorised by the permission;

(b) for requiring the removal of any building or works authorised by the permission, or the discontinuance of any use of land so authorised, at the end of a specified period, and the carrying out of any works required for the reinstatement of land at the end of that period.

Such permission granted for a limited period is known as limited permission.

Although the local planning authority may impose such conditions as they think fit, it has been decided by the courts that this power of imposing conditions must be exercised only for the purpose of the Act, i.e.

— a condition must fairly and reasonably relate to the permitted development;

— a condition must not be wholly unreasonable;

— a condition will be declared invalid if it is uncertain.

The first principle was enunciated by Lord Denning in the case Pyx Granite Ltd v. Minister of Housing and Local Government (1958 1 QB. 554 (CA), 1960 A.C. 260 (HL)), when he said that if a condition did not 'fairly and reasonably relate to the proposed operation', it would be quashed.

Another example of this principle is the case of Fawcett Properties Ltd v. Buckingham C.C. (1961 A.C. 636), where the county council had granted planning permission for two cottages in the

36

green belt subject to condition that 'the occupation of the houses shall be limited to persons whose employment or latest employment is or was employment in agriculture as defined in Section 119 of the Town and Country Planning Act 1947 (now Section 290 of the 1971 Act), or in Forestry, or in industry mainly dependent upon agriculture and including also dependants of such persons'. This condition was accepted by the House of Lords as relating to the permitted development.

The second principle is best illustrated by the case Hall and Co. Ltd. v. Shoreham-on-Sea U.D.C. (1964 1 W.L.R. 240), where a firm applied for planning permission to develop some land for industrial purposes. The land adjoined a busy main road, and in granting permission the council imposed a condition requiring the company to construct an ancillary road over their own land and to give a right of passage to the public at large. The Court of Appeal considered that the condition was unreasonable, because it required the company to construct a road and dedicate it to the public without being paid any compensation, whereas a more regular course was open to the council under Highways Acts, under which the council should acquire the land after paying proper compensation.

In another case (Kingsway Investment (Kent) Ltd v. Kent County Council 1969 (CA) 2 W.L.R. 249) the Court of Appeal considered the following condition attached to an outline planning permission: 'permission shall cease to have effect after the expiration of three years, unless within that time approval of the reversed matters has been notified to the developers'. This condition was held by the Court of Appeal to be unreasonable and invalid, because the approval and notification would be outside the control of the developer. On the other hand, when this case was considered by the House of Lords it was held that the condition was *infra vires* (i.e. valid). The House of Lords said that when the outline permission was granted under Para 5. of the General Development Order 1950, the grantee would know that he should submit details two or three months before the end of the three years' period specified in the condition, allowing two months for the authority to give or fail to give their decision and a month in which to appeal to the Minister a matter entirely within the grantee's control. This case, showing a divergence of opinion between the Court of Appeal and the House of Lords, illustrates the difficulties which may arise in the interpretation of planning permissions.

Conditions may also restrict the use of a building or limit the period of permission. Even if a change of use is permitted by the General Development Order or by the Use of Classes Order, or even if a change of use would not, in fact, be development, a condition attached to the permission may prohibit such a change (City of London Corporation v. Secretary of State for the Environment 1971 23 P & C.R. 196).

If a condition is declared invalid by the Court, the difficult problem arises, whether the whole permission is quashed, or whether the permission should stand without the condition.

This decision depends on the Court's view in each individual case, but the principle enunciated in the Kingsway Investment case, quoted above, seems to clarify the problem. The permission remains in force in spite of the quashing of a condition, if the condition relates not to development itself, but to the matter preparatory or introductory to the permission, or, in short, not important to the development itself. But this opinion should be treated with some caution, since the House of Lords indicated in the same case that in their opinion a 'time' condition was fundamental, and even if it had been void, it could not have been deleted so as to leave the permission subsisting. This last statement was, of course, *obiter*.

The local planning authority dealing with applications for planning permission is the district planning authority. Only applications in respect of developments in National Parks, or those which are contrary to the existing development plans are to be dealt with by the county planning authorities.

The Secretary of State may give direction requiring applications for planning permission to be referred to him instead of being dealt with by the local planning authority (Section 35). An example of this is the development of Piccadilly Circus in Central London, which has been 'called in' by the Secretary of State.

It should be noted that under Section 100 of the Local Government Act 1972 a local authority may arrange for discharge of any of their functions by an officer of the authority.

Appeals against Planning Decisions

If an application is made to a local planning authority to develop land, or for any approval required by the General Development Order, and the permission or approval is refused or granted subject to conditions, the aggrieved applicant may appeal to the Secretary of State (Section 36).

38

A right of appeal to the Secretary of State exists against other decisions of a local planning authority, for instance against an enforcement notice, etc.

A notice of appeal should be served within the time and in the manner prescribed by the General Development Order, i.e. in respect of appeals against planning decisions within six months.

On appeal the Secretary of State may allow or dismiss the appeal, or may reverse or vary any part of the local planning authority decision even if it was not a subject of the appeal. Thus the applicant should realise that by lodging an appeal he puts the whole issue before the Secretary of State and his decision may be even less favourable than the part of the decision which was the subject of the appeal.

This is illustrated by the case Stringer v. Minister of Housing and Local Government (Q.B.D. 1970 W.L.R.I. 1282), where the local planning authority and Manchester University signed an agreement under which the local planning authority undertook to discourage development within the limits of its powers within a specified area adjoining Jodrell Bank radio telescope. When a builder, Mr Stringer, applied for planning permission to erect 25 houses, the local planning authority refused permission on the ground that the development would interfere with the efficient running of the telescope. The Minister dismissed the appeal on the same ground. Dismissing the application for quashing the Minister's decision, the Divisional Court of the Queen's Bench Division held that the agreement between the local authority and Manchester University was without legal effect as its intention was to bind the local planning authority to disregard those considerations to which the authority was obliged to have regard under the Town and Country Planning Act. For this reason the local authority's determination was invalid, as the local authority intended to honour the agreement and this was the reason for refusal of permission. Nevertheless, the Minister had power to entertain the appeal *de novo* and the Minister had not been influenced by the agreement. 'Material considerations' (which the local authority should consider in deciding on an application) were not limited to considerations relating to amenity and, in proper case, may take into account private, as well as public, interests. The fact that the proposed development would interfere with the operation of the telescope was a material consideration.

Before deciding an appeal the Secretary of State must, on the request of either party, afford each of them an opportunity to be heard by an inspector, but the Secretary of State may, at his discretion (frequently exercised in more important appeals) order a public inquiry.

The Secretary of State may decline to determine an appeal if the planning permission should not have been granted (or granted only on the conditions complained against) in view of the provisions:

(a) relating to industrial development certificate;

(b) relating to office development permit;

(c) relating to conditions imposed by the General Development Order.

The decision of the Secretary of State is final and may be challenged in the High Court only within six weeks on a point of law.

The Secretary of State must give proper and adequate reasons for his decision, failing which his decision may be quashed in the High Court (Givaudan and Co. Ltd. v. Minister of Housing and Local Government 1967 I.W.L.R. 250).

It should be noted that under Schedule 9 to the Act some appeals of prescribed classes are determined not by the Secretary of State himself, but by a person nominated by him (i.e. by an Inspector).

The inspector (unless the Secretary of State by a direction limits the inspector's powers) determines appeals in the following matters:

(a) appeals against the decision of a planning authority refusing permission for development or granting it under conditions (Section 36 Subsections 3 and 5);

(b) appeals in respect of enforcement notice (Section 88, Subsections 4 to 6);

(c) appeals in respect of a refusal to issue an established use certificate (Section 95, Subsections 2 and 3);

(d) appeals against listed building enforcement notice (Section 97, Subsections 4 and 5);

(e) appeals against a refusal of permission or against enforcement notice in respect of tree preservation (Sections 88 and 103);

(f) appeals against a rejection of an application for listing a building as being of special historic or architectural interest (Paragraph 8 of Schedule 11).

The Secretary of State issued the 'Town and Country Planning (Determination of Appeals by Appointed Persons) (Prescribed Classes) Regulations' in 1968 (S.I. No 1972), reissued in 1970 (S.I.

40

No 1454), and again in 1972 (S.I. No 1652), which sets the following appeals against planning decisions and against enforcement notices for determination by an Inspector:

(a) the erection, or the enlargement, or other alteration of a building or buildings for use as not more than 30 dwelling houses;

(b) the development for residential purposes of land not exceeding 1 hectare in extent, where the application for planning permission does not specify the number of dwelling houses to which it relates;

(c) the erection, or the enlargement or other alteration of buildings to be used for or in connection with any of the following purposes (a shop, an office, a repository or warehouse, a hotel, boarding house, guest house, residential club, hotel or lodging house, a petrol filling station, the repair of motor vehicles or the garaging of private motor cars, religious worship or instruction or the breeding, training or keeping of dogs, cats or horses) if the aggregate floor space created by the development does not exceed 500 square metres and the area of land to which the application relates does not exceed 8,000 square metres;

(d) the formation, laying out or widening of a means of access;

(e) the carrying out of building, engineering or other operations on land for a purpose ancillary or incidental to existing or proposed development of any kind specified in the foregoing or following classes;

(f) the change in the use of a building or buildings to use as not more than 30 dwelling houses;

(g) the change in the use of a building or buildings to use for or in connection with any purpose specified in class (c) above, if the aggregate floor space used for such purpose does not exceed 500 square metres, and the area of land to which the application relates does not exceed 8,000 square metres.

Appeals in the following five categories will, however, be decided by the Secretary of State:

(a) if the application has been the subject of a direction by the Secretary of State for the Environment or the Ministry of Transport;

(b) if the appeal has been made by a local authority or a statutory undertaker;

(c) if the local planning authority refused permission or imposed conditions because of the views expressed by a Government

41

Department or a New Town Corporation;

(d) if another appeal or application relating to the same development is concurrently being considered by the Secretary of State;

(e) if another appeal or application not within the classes entrusted to the inspector, but relating to the same land is concurrently considered by the Secretary of State.

The Secretary of State can at any time by means of Regulation or Direction remove some classes of appeals entrusted to the Inspector and take over himself.

Any inspector who becomes empowered to determine an appeal is afforded the same powers and duties as the Secretary of State. The parties should be asked by the Inspector whether they wish to be heard and if they do, they must be afforded at least a private hearing. The Inspector may hold a public inquiry before he decides the appeal, and must do so, if instructed by the Secretary of State. When the appeal is decided by the Inspector his decision becomes equivalent to that of the Secretary of State.

The Secretary of State has power to substitute one Inspector for another or to restore the responsibility for individual decision to himself. The substituted Inspector must begin his consideration afresh, but it is not necessary to give any person the opportunity either of making fresh representations or to modify or withdraw representations already made.

Duration of Planning Permission (Sections 41-44)

The 1962 Act provided that, without prejudice to any revocation or modification of planning permission, permission once granted, should enure for the benefit of land for ever, unless the local planning authority attached a condition that the permitted operation should start within a given time, or permitted change of use should take place within a specified period (Kingsway Investment (Kent) Ltd v. Kent County Council (1968) 3 All E.R. 197; (CA) 1969 2 W.L.R. 249).

Now, however, there are two limitations in time:

— the permitted development must start within the statutory time;

— if the completion of the development is unduly delayed, the local planning authority may issue a 'completion notice'.

The general provision is, that every permitted development must begin not later than the expiration of five years or within such a shorter period, as the local planning authority may impose as a condition in granting the permission.

As, however, this provision was introduced by the 1968 Act for the first time, development permitted before the commencement of the 1968 Act should begin within five years since the Act came into operation (this part of the Act came into operation on 1 April 1969).

The development is deemed to begin if a 'specified operation' has been carried out. 'Specified operation', which is widely defined, involves any of the following:

(a) any work of construction in the course of the erection of a building;

(b) the digging of a trench which is to contain the foundations, or part of the foundations, of a building;

(c) the laying of any underground main or pipe to the foundations, or part of the foundations, of a building;

(d) any operation in the course of laying out or constructing a road or part of a road;

(e) any change in the use of any land, where that change constitutes a material development.

In respect to outline planning permission, an application for the approval of reserved matters must be made within three years; the development itself must start either within five years from the granting of the outline planning permission, or within two years of the approval of the reserved matters, whichever is the later.

It is possible, however, that the developer may start the development within the time prescribed by the Act or by the condition attached to the permission, but does not proceed with the works, leaving them unfinished for a considerable time.

To avoid this unsatisfactory situation, Section 44 provides that if the local planning authority are of the opinion that the development will not be completed within a reasonable time, they may serve a notice — called a completion notice — stating that the permission will cease to have effect at the expiration of a further reasonable time, being not less than 12 months after the notice takes effect.

A completion notice should be served on the owner and other persons, who may be affected by the notice. For its validity it requires confirmation by the Secretary of State, who may substitute a longer period for completion of the works in question. After receiving a completion notice any person may require to be heard by

43

a Department's Inspector and the Secretary of State has to arrange such a hearing before confirming the completion notice. If the completion notice is not complied with, the permission for development ceases to have effect. The local authority, however, is authorised to withdraw a completion notice even if it has been confirmed.

Revocation or Modification of Planning Permission (Sections 45-46)

The local planning authority may at any time revoke or modify the planning permission granted by them, but such a revocation may be exercised only before the operation permitted has been completed or before the permitted change of use has taken place.

Such revocation or modification requires confirmation by the Secretary of State, unless the persons concerned agree in writing to the revocation and it appears to the authority that no claim for compensation is likely to arise. If the planning permission is revoked or modified, the local planning authority has a duty to pay a compensation to the person interested in the land, who has incurred expenditure in carrying out work which is rendered abortive by the revocation or modification or who has otherwise sustained loss or damage which is directly attributable to the revocation or modification (Section 164).

Planning Inquiry Commission (Sections 47-50)

The Secretary of State has power to constitute a Planning Inquiry Commission. Such a Commission consists of a chairman and between two to four members.

Matters may be referred to the Planning Inquiry Commission if they are considered of national or regional importance, or if technical or scientific aspects of the proposed development are of so unfamiliar character as to prejudice a proper determination, in the absence of a special inquiry for the purpose.

The following four matters may be referred to the Planning Inquiry Commission:

(a) any application for planning permission, which the Secretary of State called in for decision by himself;

(b) any appeal against a planning decision;

(c) any proposal under Section 40 in respect of some development by statutory undertakers;

(d) any proposal that development should be carried by or on behalf of a government department.

The duty of the Planning Inquiry Commission falls under the following three headings:

(a) to identify and investigate the technical or scientific problems relevant to the question whether the proposed development should be permitted;

(b) to afford interested persons (and the local authority) an opportunity to appear before one or more members of the Commission;

(c) to report to the responsible Minister on the matter referred to them. Thus the Planning Inquiry Commission acts exclusively in an advisory capacity and has no authority to decide the issue.

Discontinuance of Use or Alteration or Removal of Buildings or Works (Sections 51-52)

The planning authority has yet another power of control which is probably the most far-reaching. It can issue an order (which has to be approved by the Secretary of State) requiring the discontinuance of any use of land and building or removal or alteration of any building or works, even if the existing use or operation has been effected with full legality. In such a case, however, full compensation will be paid by the local planning authority issuing the order and for this reason it may be assumed that this kind of power will be used extremely cautiously.

Special Provisions in Respect of Conservation Areas

Until the Civic Amenities Act 1967 only individual buildings had been subject to preservation, but this Act created a new concept 'conservation areas'. The provisions of the Civic Amenities Act 1967, as far as they referred to town and country planning problems were incorporated into the Town and Country Planning Act 1971. Thus under Section 277 'it is a duty of every local planning authority to determine which part of their area are areas of special architectural or historic interest, the character or appearance of which it is desirable to preserve or enhance, and shall designate such areas as conservation areas'. The Secretary of State may direct a local planning authority to designate an area as a conservation area. Designation of conservation area should be notified to the Secretary of State and published in the *London Gazette* and at least one local newspaper. There are now well over 1500 conservation areas in this country.

There is a number of special provisions in the Town and Country Planning Act in respect of conservation areas, the most important being:

Any application for development, which, in the opinion of the local planning authority would affect the character or appearance of a conservation area must be published by a notice advertised in a local newspaper and displayed on the site and members of the public can raise objection to the application.

The Secretary of State is authorised to give directions to local planning authorities as to the matters which they must consider when dealing with such an application, and as to the consultation with persons or bodies, which ought to take place before a decision is made.

The Town and Country Planning (Amendment) Act 1972 gives the local planning authority power of control over demolition of any building in conservation areas, even if they are not listed buildings (Section 8 of the 1972 Act). The local planning authority may issue a direction that a building or buildings in the conservation area be subject to such a control. The direction requires confirmation by the Secretary of State. Detailed provisions in respect of the control over buildings in conservation areas (and buildings of special historic or architectural interest) are contained in the Town and Country Planning (Listed Buildings and Buildings in Conservation Areas) Regulations 1972 (S.I. 1362).

Chapter 6

ADDITIONAL CONTROL IN SPECIAL CASES

Buildings of Special Architectural or Historic Interest (Sections 54-58)

In order to assist local planning authorities in considering buildings of special architectural or historic interest, the Secretary of State compiles a list of such buildings. In listing the buildings the Secretary of State takes into account not only the building itself, but also questions of contribution to the historic or architectural interest of any group of buildings, and the desirability of preserving any feature of the building or its curtilage. A copy of the list is supplied to councils of the county boroughs and county districts and the owners and occupiers of the buildings in question are notified. The listing of a building is also noted in the local land charges register.

The legal consequence of listing is that any act causing damage to a listed building is an offence punishable by a fine.

Even if a building is not listed, the local planning authority may issue a 'building preservation notice' which is valid for six months, and which has the same effect as if the building had been listed. The Secretary of State may list the building within the six months, but if the building is not listed within that period, the building preservation notice becomes ineffective.

It is an offence to demolish, alter or extend a listed building without obtaining a 'listed building consent'. This should be distinguished from the normal planning permission, which may not be necessary according to the provisions of Part III of the Act. Although so far as general planning control is concerned it is an open question whether demolition of a building is a development, demolition of a listed building requires 'listed building consent'.

Ancient monuments and churches (but not parsonage houses) are exempted from the provisions of this part of the Act.

If the listed building has become incapable of reasonably beneficial use in its existing state, and listed building consent is refused, the owner may serve on the local authority a 'listed building purchase notice', requiring the local authority to buy the building.

The local authority or the Secretary of State may acquire compulsorily any listed building which is not being properly preserved, but this may be done only after a 'repair notice' has been ineffective for at least one month. The compensation paid is assessed according to normal rules of compensation, but the depreciating factor that the building is listed is not taken into account. If, however, it is established that the building has been deliberately allowed to fall into disrepair, then a 'minimum compensation' is payable, which excludes any profit which may arise from the possibility of the development of the site.

Schedule 19 provides for the procedure on application for a listed building consent. The procedure is also governed by the Town and Country Planning (Listed Buildings and Buildings in Conservation Areas) Regulations 1972 (S.I. 1362) which revoked and re-enacted with amendments the previous Regulations of 1968 (S.I. 1910). The Regulations apply to listed buildings and to the buildings in conservation areas, which are the subject of a direction under Section 8 of the Town and Country Planning Act 1972.[1] The Regulations prescribe the manner in which applications for listed building consent are to be made and advertised, and the manner in which appeals may be made by persons aggrieved by decisions of local planning authorities; prescribe the manner in which claims are to be made for compensation arising from the application of listed building control, the serving of listed building purchase notice, the advertising of unopposed orders revoking or modifying listed building consents and the execution of works under listed building enforcement procedure; and prescribe form of notices to owners and occupiers of buildings which become listed or which have ceased to be listed.

Trees (Sections 59-62)

In granting planning permission the local planning authority must ensure, whenever it is appropriate, that a condition for the preservation or planting of trees is made.

In addition the authority has a duty to issue a 'tree preservation order' if it is in the interest of the amenity to preserve a single tree, a group of trees or a woodland. Such an order may make provisions for:

(a) the prohibition of the cutting down, topping, lopping or wilful destruction of trees except with the consent of the local authority;

(b) the securing of re-planting of trees.

It is permitted to fell trees which are subject to an order, if the trees in question are dead, dying or dangerous, or insofar as they are a nuisance. In case of nuisance, the applicant must prove not merely inconvenience, but inevitable and imminent damage to premises (Edgeborough Building Co. Ltd. v. Woking U.D.C. 1966 Estate Gazette of 4th May 1966).

An application to a local authority for any consent in respect of tree preservation follows the procedure for usual planning application with a few exceptions, e.g. there is never a necessity to give publicity to the application.[2] A purchase notice may be served in respect of land being subject to a tree preservation order in similar circumstances as in other planning decisions.

If a local authority intends to make a Tree Preservation Order it must serve a copy of the order upon owners and occupiers of the land affected. The persons interested may submit objections within 28 days, and these are sent to the Secretary of State if any objections are made. If no objections are made, the local authority may confirm the order. Contravention of a tree preservation order is an offence punishable by a fine.

Advertisements

Section 290 defines advertisements very widely, as 'any word, letter, model, sign, placard, board, notice, device or representation, whether illuminated or not, in the nature of, and employed wholly or partly for the purpose of advertisement, announcement or direction, and (without prejudice to the preceeding provisions of the definition) includes any hoarding or similar structure used, or adapted for use, for the display of advertisements, and references to the display of advertisements shall be construed accordingly'.

Regulations issued under Section 63 of the Act[3] restrict and regulate the display of advertisements.

Some advertisements, however, are excluded from the operation of the Regulations and are, as such, not subject to any control of advertisements:

(a) on land enclosed by a hedge, fence, wall or similar screen or structure, where the advertisements are not readily visible from outside the enclosure;

(b) inside a building and not visible from the outside;

(c) on or in moving vehicles; (d) incorporated in and forming part of the fabric of a building; but an advertisement does not become part of the fabric of the building by merely being affixed or painted on;

(e) displayed on an article for sale or on its packet or container.

Regulation 9 also allows the following three types of advertisements ('deemed consent'.):

(a) pending parliamentary or local government elections;

(b) advertisements displayed under statutory obligations;

(c) advertisements in the nature of traffic signs.

Six classes of advertisements enumerated in Regulation 14 may be displayed without obtaining an express consent from the local planning authority, but the authority may serve a notice of discontinuance if it considered to be expedient in the interest of amenity or public safety.

Class I

This class comprises the functional advertisements of local authorities, statutory undertakers and public transport undertakers. Examples of these advertisements are 'bus stop signs, signs indicating the way to railway stations, etc.

Class II

It includes miscellaneous advertisements relating to the premises on which they are displayed and includes, e.g., advertisements for the purpose of identification, direction or warning, advertisements relating to a person or firm carrying on a profession, business or trade at the premises, etc.

Class III

This class includes certain advertisements of a temporary nature, e.g. 'for sale', 'to let' boards, etc.

Class IV

This class comprises advertisements displayed on business premises wholly with reference to the following matters: the business carried on, the goods or service provided, the name and qualifications of the persons carrying on such business or activity or supplying such goods or services on those premises.

Class V

This class comprises advertisements displayed on any forecourt of business premises with reference to the matter specified in Class IV.

Class VI

This class comprises advertisements in the form of a flag attached to an upright flagstaff, fixed on the roof of the advertiser's building and bearing his name and device only.

All these advertisements are limited in their sizes and the limits are indicated separately for each group.

Advertisements which were displayed on 1 August 1948 are called 'existing advertisements' and are also permitted without the necessity of obtaining an express consent.

Even if the advertisement is not subject to consent, the local planning authority may 'challenge' it, which means that the authority may require that even such an advertisement shall be subject to application and consent. The local planning authority must give full reasons why, in the interest of amenity, such consent is required. Challenging procedure is not allowed in respect of advertisements allowed by Regulation 9, as those are displayed in the public interest.

Section 63 allows the regulations to define 'areas of special control' being either rural areas, or other areas requiring special provisions in order to preserve amenity. In such areas advertisements may be either completely disallowed, or allowed within special limits imposed by the regulations.

An application for express consent should be made in London to the London Boroughs, elsewhere to the county borough councils (until they will cease to exist on 1 April 1974 when the Local Government Act 1972 comes into operation) or county district council. After 1 April 1974 all applications should be submitted to the district planning authority.

The authority may either grant consent or refuse it. Every grant must be for a fixed term, which may exceed five years only with the consent of the Secretary of State.

An applicant for express consent who is aggrieved by the decision of the local planning authority may appeal to the Secretary of State within one month from the receipt of notification. The decision of the Secretary of State is final, but may be challenged in the High Court within six weeks on the point of law only.

Any person displaying an advertisement so as to contravene the Regulations is liable to a fine, and if the offence is continuing after conviction, for a further daily fine.

Waste Land (Section 65)

If it appears to a local planning authority that the amenity of their area is seriously injured by the condition of any garden, vacant site or other open land, then the authority may serve on the owner and occupier of the land a notice requiring the abatement of the injury within a specified period.

If the requirement is not complied with, an enforcement notice can be served by the local planning authority as in cases of other contraventions of planning control.

Industrial Development (Sections 66-72)

'Industrial building' means a building used for the making of any article, for the altering, repairing, ornamenting, adopting for sale, etc. of any article, for getting, dressing or preparation for sale of minerals or the extraction or preparation for sale of oil and brine. Any building used or designed for the carrying on of scientific research is also included into the definition. Also a building providing ancillary services is included.

With some exceptions mentioned in Subsection 5 of Section 67 and in Section 68 any application to the local planning authority for permission to develop land by the erection of an industrial building shall be of no effect, unless an Industrial Development Certificate is issued by the Secretary of State. Such a Certificate must state that the development is consistent with the proper distribution of industry and a particular regard should be paid to the need for providing appropriate employment in development areas.

An Industrial Development Certificate shall not be required:

(a) for the extension of an industrial building if the extension taken by itself would not be an industrial building;

(b) for retention of a building or continuance of use of land after the end of any period specified only in planning permission and not in an Industrial Development Certificate;

(c) for the erection of an industrial building if the floor space created by the development does not exceed 5,000 square feet; this limit may be lowered by an order of the Secretary of State (for some parts of the country the limit has been lowered to 3,000 square feet);

(d) for the extension for industrial purposes of an industrial building by floor space not exceeding 5,000 square feet.

An Industrial Development Certificate may impose conditions which the Secretary of State considers appropriate having regard to the proper distribution of industry. The scope of these conditions is much more extensive than the scope of planning conditions and in particular the conditions can:

(a) require the removal of any building or the discontinuance of any use of land at the end of a specified period;

(b) restrict the amount of office floor space in any building to which the certificate relates.

Although the local planning authority cannot consider an application which is not supported by an Industrial Development Certificate, they must consider whether they would have given permission if the certificate had been obtained. If they would not have given permission they must notify the applicant accordingly and in such case the absence of the Industrial Development Certificate will not prevent the applicant from obtaining compensation for refusal of planning permission or a serving of a purchase notice.

Office Development (Sections 73-86)

These provisions of the Act were originally valid until 5 August 1972, as they were enacted for seven years by the Control of Office and Industrial Development Act 1965 and are now incorporated into the Town and Country Planning Act 1971. They have since been extended for a further period of five years.

The provisions apply to South-East England only, but may be extended to such other areas as may be designated by the Secretary of State.

Where the provisions apply, an application for planning permission for the provision of new offices, whether by the erection or extension of buildings or by the change of use, must be accompanied by an Office Development Permit issued by the Secretary of State. An Office Development Permit is not required if the development in question does not exceed 10,000 square feet. In issuing a certificate the Secretary of State has much the same powers to impose conditions as in the case of an Industrial Development Certificate.

Caravans

Use of land as a caravan site is of considerable importance from the point of view of planning, because these sites, if not properly established and maintained, may become detrimental to the amenity of the neighbourhood. For this reason caravan sites are subject to dual control. In the first instance the developer must obtain planning permission for the establishment of a site for caravans (it will usually be development involving material change of use of the land), but, in addition, he is required to obtain afterwards a 'site licence' under the Caravan Sites and Control of Development Act 1960. A contravention of this requirement is an offence punishable by a fine.

The local authorities responsible for the issue of 'site licence' are not planning, but housing authorities, i.e. district councils. If planning permission has been granted for the use of land as a caravan site, the local authority must issue a site licence; thus the real significance of the site licence is not whether it could be granted or not — as it must be granted if planning permission has been given — but the possibility of imposing conditions attached to the site licence.

These conditions must be such as the authority considers necessary or desirable to impose in the interest of:

(a) caravan dwellers on the site itself;

(b) any other class of persons (e.g. neighbours);

(c) the public at large (Section 5(1) of the Caravans Sites and Control of Development Act 1960).

Apart from any conditions, which the local authority may impose, the Act specifically authorises the imposition of the following conditions:

(a) for restricting the occasions on which caravans are stationed on land for human habitation, or the total number of caravans which are so stationed at any one time;

(b) for controlling the types of caravans which are stationed on land;

(c) for regulating the position in which caravans are stationed on land for human habitation and for prohibiting, restricting or otherwise regulating the placing or erection on such land, at any time when caravans are so stationed, of structures and vehicles of any description whatsoever and of tents;

(d) for securing the amenity of land, including the planting of trees and bushes;

54

(e) for securing fire precautions;

(f) for securing that adequate sanitary facilities and other facilities are provided for the use of persons dwelling in caravans.

If the developer is aggrieved by the condition attached to the site licence, he may appeal to the magistrates' court within 28 days.

There are some minor exceptions from the requirement to obtain a site licence (Section 2 of the 1960 Act and First Schedule).

Chapter 7

LOCAL PLANNING AUTHORITIES IN
PLANNING CONTROL

The Local Government Act 1972[1] which comes into operation on 1 April 1974 allocates the responsibility for planning control to both county and district councils.

Some applications, orders or notices in planning may relate to 'county matters'. 'County matter' means (Para 32 of the 16th Schedule to the Local Government Act 1972):

(a) the winning and working of minerals or the erection of buildings for use in this connection;

(b) searches and tests of mineral deposits;

(c) the use of land for disposing of mineral waste;

(d) any development which:

— would conflict with the structure plan,

— would conflict with the old style development plan if in existence,

— would be inconsistent with a local plan,

— would be inconsistent with any statement of policy adopted by the county council;

(e) a development affecting a National Park;

f) any development or class of developments prescribed by the Secretary of State by regulation as being a county matter.

The general principle is reasonably simple. Application for:

(a) planning permission in respect of general planning control;

(b) determinations under Section 53 whether such a permission is required;

(c) an established use certificate under Section 94;

are to be decided by the district planning authority, unless the application pertains to the county matter as defined above, in which case it will be decided by the county planning authority. If county planning authorities are determining an application for planning permission they should afford the district planning authority an opportunity to make recommendations.

District planning authorities are responsible for:

(a) the revocation of modification of planning permission (Section 45);

the issuing of an order requiring a discontinuance of use (Section 51);

the imposing of conditions on continuance of use, the requiring of alterations or removal of buildings;

(b) the serving of enforcement notices or stop notices.

If the above notices or orders refer to county matters, the county planning authority should be consulted first. In respect of county matters, moreover, both local authorities (county and district) have the above jurisdiction.

It is also a district planning authority's responsibility:

(c) to maintain a register of planning applications and decisions (Section 34);

(d) to deal with listed buildings (Sections 55, 56, 96, 99 and Schedule 11), including enforcement procedure and to issue building preservation notices, and to be concerned with the control of advertisements.

If the Secretary of State so directs, the planning authority dealing with points (c) and (d) has to obtain specialist advice in connection with the exercise of these functions.

Other functions are, generally speaking, within the jurisdiction of both county and district authorities. Detailed allocation is given in Schedule 16 to the Local Government Act 1972.

A local highway authority will be able to impose restrictions on the grant by the local planning authority of planning permission in respect of means of access to a classified road, and also where the development in question appears to increase the volume of traffic.

Chapter 8

ENFORCEMENT OF CONTROL

General[1]

Where it appears to the local planning authority (usually the district council — see Chapter 7) that there has been a breach of planning control after the end of 1963, then the local authority, if it considers it expedient to do so, having regard to the provisions of the development plan and to any other material consideration, may serve an 'enforcement notice' under the Act, requiring the breach to be remedied.

It is of interest to note that the local planning authority should not automatically serve an enforcement notice in respect of any breach of planning control. They should be satisfied that it is desirable to serve a notice having regard to the provisions of the development plan and other material considerations. The planning authority should consider whether they would have granted planning permission had an application been made to them. Only if they take the view that they would not have granted permission, should they serve the enforcement notice.

It should be recognised that breach of planning contol is not a criminal offence; it is only the non-compliance with an enforcement notice which is punishable.

'Four Years Rule'

Section 87 states that only a breach of planning control which has occurred after the end of 1963 may be subject to an enforcement notice. This is so because, under the 1947 and 1962 Acts, any authorised development could not be a subject to an enforcement notice if four years had expired since the breach. But the 1968 Act changed this in respect of some developments effected after the end of 1963 (as those developments which took place before the end of 1963 could not be challenged because they become legalised by the 'four years rule' before the 1968 Act came into operation). Now the four years rule applies only to certain developments.

If the enforcement notice relates to a breach of planning control consisting of:

(a) the carrying on without planning permission of building, engineering, mining or other operations in, on, over or under the land;

(b) the failure to comply with any condition or limitation which relates to the above development;

(c) the making without permission of a change of use of any building to use as a single dwelling house,

it may be served only within the period of four years from the date of breach.

Thus the four years rule has been retained in respect of all operations (including conditions imposed in connection with these permissions) and one change of use, and has been abolished — as far as development had taken place after 1963 — in respect of all other changes of use.

Enforcement Notice

An enforcement notice is served on the owner and on the occupier of the land and on any other person having an interest in the land, being an interest which is, in the opinion of the authority, materially affected by the notice. An enforcement notice may also be served if a condition imposed in the planning has been broken.

An enforcement notice should specify:

(a) the matters alleged to constitute a breach of planning control;

(b) the steps required by the authority to remedy the breach;

(c) the period for compliance with the notice, i.e. the period (beginning with the date when the notice takes effect) within which those steps are requested to be taken.

An enforcement notice becomes effective at the end of such period, not being less than 28 days after the service of the notice, as may be specified in the notice. Thus the notice specifies two periods: first, the one in which it takes effect, and the second the one within which the notice should be complied with.

An enforcement notice which does not comply with the above requirements is invalid. Thus if it does not specify two periods (when the notice becomes operative and when it should be complied with) or if it is ambiguous and uncertain in its allegations and in indicating steps required to be taken by the applicant, it will be null and void (Burgess v. Jarvis and Sevenoaks R.D.C. (1952) 1 All E.R. 592).

The local planning authority may withdraw the enforcement notice at any time before it takes effect.

Appeals against Enforcement Notice
Persons on whom the enforcement notice has been served, or any other interested person may appeal to the Secretary of State for the Environment within the period specified in the enforcement notice as the period at the end of which it is to take effect. The appeal may be made on the following and only on the following grounds:

(a) that planning permission ought to be granted for the development in question or that the condition imposed ought to be disregarded;

(b) that the matters alleged in the notice do not constitute a breach of planning control;

(c) that the four years rule should have been applied and the notice has been served after the development became unassailable;

(d) in other cases, that the development in question was carried out before the beginning of 1964;

(e) that the enforcement notice was not served as required by the Act;

(f) that the steps required to be taken by the enforcement notice exceed that which is necessary to remedy the breach of planning control;

(g) that the period specified for compliance with the enforcement notice is too short.

An appeal should indicate the grounds for the appeal and the facts on which it is based. On any such appeal the Secretary of State shall, if either the appellant or the local planning authority so desire, afford to each of them an opportunity of appearing before an Inspector nominated by the Secretary of State.

The enforcement notice does not take effect until the final determination or the withdrawal of the appeal, and the period given for compliance with the notice starts to run only when the notice becomes thus effective.

The Secretary of State on receiving an appeal may:

(a) correct any informality, defect or error in the enforcement

60

notice if he is satisfied that they are not material;

(b) if the ground of an appeal is the fact that the notice was not served on a person, he may disregard it if neither the appellant nor that person have been substantially prejudiced by this error.

If the appeal only concerns the above problems it does not require to be determined.

On the determination of an appeal the Secretaty of State shall, in addition to deciding the appeal, issue directions for giving effect to his decision, either by quashing the enforcement notice or by varying its terms. He may also:

(a) grant planning permission for the development to which the enforcement notice refers, or discharge any condition;

(b) determine any purpose for which the land may be lawfully used, having regard to any past use and to planning permission relating to the land.

In considering whether to grant planning permission the Secretary of State must pay attention to the provisions of the development plan and to any other material consideration.

Any planning permission granted by the secretary of State as a result of an appeal against an enforcement notice (and this appeal is treated also as an application for planning permission for development being subject to the enforcement notice) may be granted subject to conditions.

If the Secretary of State on appeal discharges a condition or limitation, he may substitute another condition or limitation, whether less or more onerous. Any planning decision issued by the Secretary of State is final.

Although the decision of the Secretary of State is final, the appellant, the local planning authority or any other person on whom the enforcement notice has been served, may either appeal against the decision to the High Court on a point of law, or require the Secretary of State to state a case for the opinion of the High Court.

If an enforcement notice is alleged to be not only 'invalid' but 'null and void' (*ultra vires*), the appellant instead of exercising his right of appeal to the Secretary of State may proceed in the Court for a declaratory judgement. It was by this procedure that the two leading cases: Pyx Granite Co. (1959 3 All E.R. 1) and Fawcett Properties Ltd (1960 3 All E.R. 303) about the conditions attached to the planning permission were decided.

Appeals against enforcement notices may be decided by a person nominated by the Secretaty of State (i.e. by an Inspector), as explained in Chapter 3.

Penalties for Non-compliance with the Enforcement Notice

Under Section 89 any person who, at the time when the notice was served on him, was the owner of the land to which it relates and who has not taken the steps required by the notice (other than discontinuance of a use of land) within the period allowed for compliance, shall be liable to a fine. A fine on summary conviction shall not exceed £400, but on conviction on indictment it may be of unlimited amount.

Where an enforcement notice requires the discontinuance of use of land, then, if any person uses the land in contravention of the notice, he will be liable to similar fines as above, but in addition he may be subject to a daily penalty of £50 on summary conviction or an unlimited fine on conviction on indictment.

If a person, having been convicted for non-compliance. with an enforcement notice, fails to do everything in his power to comply with the notice as soon as is practicable, he is liable to a further daily penalty of £50 on summary conviction or of an unlimited amount on conviction on indictment.

Stop Notice and its Consequences

The enforcement notice becomes operative only if the appeal and other legal proceedings challenging it have been disposed of. This means that the person on whom an enforcement notice has been served could (until the 1968 Act) protract an unauthorised development by vexatious appeals. The 1968 Act (now Section 90 of the 1971 Act) introduced a new device, the 'Stop Notice', the effect of which is to stop the carrying out of some developments almost immediately. The stop notice may refer to any operation, but not to a change of use, unless the alleged breach of planning control is the deposit of waste materials, in which case a stop notice may be issued. Thus a stop notice may be issued when the development is irreversible, or could be reversed only at great cost and trouble.

The local planning authority may serve a stop notice, once the enforcement notice has been served, in respect of one of the developments described above. The stop notice must refer to the enforcement notice and the enforcement notice must be attached to the stop notice.

A stop notice may be served on any person who appears to the local authority to have an interest in the land, or to be concerned with the carrying out of any operation on the land. Thus the stop notice may be served on the contractor carrying out the operation which is subject to the stop notice.

The stop notice prohibits any person on whom it is served from carrying out or even continuing any specific operation on the land, to which the enforcement notice relates, which are either covered by the enforcement notice as being in breach of planning control, or are operations so closely associated with such operation as to constitute substantially the same operation.

A stop notice:

(a) must specify the date on which it is to take effect and this may be not earlier than three, and not later than 14 days from the date on which it is first served on any person;

(b) in relation to any person served it will take effect on the date specified, but not earlier than three days from the date of serving;

(c) is related to the enforcement notice and ceases to have effect when the enforcement notice is withdrawn or quashed. It is also repealed automatically when the enforcement notice takes effect, as then it is no longer necessary.

There is no appeal against the stop notice. Failure to comply with a stop notice involves the same penalties as failure to comply with an enforcement notice.

The stop notice can have serious consequences for the person affected; in building contracts it may involve heavy losses for the contractor. Since there is no defence against a stop notice, compensation may be due (see Chapter 13).

Established use Certificate

The partial abolition of the four years rule discussed at the beginning of this chapter, means that in cases where the four years rule has been abolished (i.e. in cases of all changes of use, with the exception of the conversion of a building into a single dwelling house), developments effected before the end of 1963 were already authorised at the moment when the rule was abolished, whereas those which have been carried out after 1 January 1964 have been caught by the abolition of the rule. For this reason it is essential to know whether the change of use in question took place before the end of 1963 or after, as only the latter can be challenged by the local planning authority.

If in the future such a dispute arises, it may be extremely difficult, if not impossible, to decide whether the development, being carried out either before or after the end of 1963, is authorised or not. For this reason the Act, in Sections 94 and 95, provides for a certificate of established use.

A use of land may, on application, be certified by a local planning authority as an established use, in which event the applicant is entitled to receive from the local planning authority an 'established use certificate'.

A use of land established if:

(a) it was begun before the beginning of 1964 without planning permission and has continued since the end of 1964; or

(b) it was begun before the beginning of 1964 under a planning permission granted subject to conditions or limitations, which have not been complied with since the end of 1963; or

(c) it was begun after the end of 1963 as a result of a change of use not requiring planning permission and there has been no change of use requiring planning permission since the end of 1963 (change of use of a building into a single dwelling house cannot be certified, as such a change is still subject to the four years rule).

An established use certificate may be granted either by a local planning authority or by the Secretary of State. It may be done either if he directs that a certificate would be issued by him ('called in application') or an appeal against the local authority's decision refusing the issue of a certificate.

If, on the application for a certificate, the local planning authority is satisfied that the claim has been made out, they must grant him the certificate. Otherwise they must refuse it.

The detailed provisions as to the method of applying for the certificate, of appealing against the refusal and as to the form of a certificate are given in Schedule 14 to the Act.

An established use certificate is conclusive evidence in any appeal against an enforcement notice and it is, therefore, an important document. False or reckless statement made by the applicant in order to obtain a certificate is an offence punishable by a fine on summary conviction.

ENFORCEMENT PROCEDURE IN SPECIAL CASES

Listed Buildings

Contravention of provisions in respect of control over listed buildings may be the subject of a 'listed building enforcement notice' under Sections 96-101 of the Act. The notice is subject to appeal to the Secretary of State and the grounds of appeal are similar to those in the normal enforcement procedure, with the additional ground that the building is not of special architectural or historic interest although listed, or that the works were urgently necessary in the interest of safety or health, or preservation of the building.

In the event of non-compliance with the notice the local planning authority may recover penalties from the person in default, or may themselves take steps to implement the enforcement notice. The costs of these steps may be recovered from the offender.

Trees

If any person, in contravention of a Tree Preservation Order, cuts down or wilfully destroys a tree, or tops or lops a tree, he is liable to a fine, and a further daily fine for continuing the offence after the conviction (Sections 102-103).

In addition, the local planning authority may within four years from the date of failure to comply with the Tree Preservation Order, serve on the owner of the land a notice requiring him to replant a tree or trees of such size and species as may be specified, within a stated period. There is a right of appeal to the Secretary of State against the notice demanding the replacement of trees. If the notice is not complied with the local planning authority may do the work themselves and recover the costs from the offender.

Waste Land

If a notice in respect of waste land, issued under Section 65 is not complied with, the offender is liable to a fine (Sections 104-107). There is a right of appeal against the notice in respect of waste land to the Magistrates' Court with a further appeal to the Crown Court. If the notice is not complied with, the local planning authority may enter the land and take the necessary steps, recovering the costs from the offender.

Other Controls

An order under Section 51, instructing the discontinuance of an authorised use or alteration or removal of authorised buildings and works is also subject to enforcement (Sections 108-109). Non-compliance with the order is a summary offence and in addition the local planning authority may take steps to alter or remove the building, recovering the costs from the offender.

Similar provisions exist in respect of the unauthorised display of advertisements.

Chapter 9

PLANNING INQUIRIES

It has been noted that in many instances, where the action of a local planning authority is challenged by a person, the aggrieved person is entitled, before the final decision is taken, to ask for a hearing before a person appointed by the Secretary of State. It is within the discretion of the Secretary of State to order a public inquiry instead of granting a hearing. A public inquiry may take place if objections are made against the proposed development plan (whether a structure plan or local plan), if an appeal is lodged against a decision of a local planning authority refusing permission for development, or granting of it subject to conditions or limitations, if a local planning authority issues an enforcement notice and in other cases.

The procedure of the planning inquiry in respect of appeals is now governed by two statutory instruments: where the issue being the subject of the inquiry is to be determined by the Secretary of State himself, it is now governed by the Rules issued in 1969 (Town and Country Planning (Inquiry procedure) Rules 1969 S.I. No. 1092); where the appeal is to be determined by the Inspector the Rules of 1968 apply (Town and Country Planning Appeals (Determination by Appointed Persons) (Inquiry Procedure) Rules 1968 S.I. No. 1952). The procedure is similar in either case up to the close of the Inquiry.

Not later than 28 days before the inquiry the local planning authority must send a written statement concerning its case to the appellant and to every 'Section 29 party'. 'Section 29 parties' are persons who, being estate owners have been notified about the application according to Section 27, who have made representations in the case where the application was advertised in the local newspaper, e.g. in case of 'bad neighbour' developments, who are agricultural tenants or who made representations in respect of an application for development in a conservation area.

The statement of the local planning authority must contain the following:

(a) a statement of the submission which the authority proposes to put forward at the inquiry;

(b) a list of all documents to which the authority intends to refer at the inquiry. All interested parties must be allowed to examine these documents;

(c) any relevant direction given by the Secretary of State or the Minister of Transport and a copy of the direction and the reason given for their making;

(d) any expression of views given by any Government Department on which the authority proposes to rely.

The local planning authority must not depart from their statement without the leave of the Inspector conducting the inquiry.

The Secretary of State may also require the applicant to supply a written statement of the submission which he proposes to put forward to the inquiry and a list of documents. Here again the appellant must obtain the leave of the Inspector if he wishes to depart from his statement. Thus a statement of the local authority is obligatory, whereas the appellant has to submit his statements only if instructed to do so by the Inspector.

The procedure at the inquiry is as follows:

The Inspector opens the proceedings by stating the purpose of the inquiry. The appellant and the local authority 'enter their appearance' either personally or by an advocate (solicitor, barrister or professional representative).

It is usually the appellant who opens the case and calls the witnesses. Although witnesses may be required to make their deposition on oath, in practice this is done only in appeals against enforcement notice and rarely in other appeals. The rules of evidence are much less strictly applied than in a court of law. Even hearsay evidence may be allowed, although the Inspector may disregard it. Each witness may expect to be cross-examined by the representative of the local planning authority and by any Section 29 party. Other interested persons may ask questions by the leave of the Inspector.

The appellant may also produce letters and other documents.

Afterwards the local planning authority puts its case in a similar manner, and the same right to ask questions is available to Section 29 parties.

The appellant makes his final speech, and afterwards the

Inspector usually visits the site in the company of the representatives of both parties.

If the case is to be decided by the Inspector, he notifies his decision with reasons to the appellant, local planning authority and section 29 parties. If he intends to take new evidence, not revealed during the inquiry, he must notify the parties, who are entitled to make further representations within 21 days.

If the decision lies with the Secretary of State, the Inspector submits his report with his conclusions. Usually he makes recommendations, but he may refrain from doing so, giving reason for so doing. The Secretary of State may disagree with the Inspector on findings of fact and then no additional inquiry is ordered. Only the appellant, the local authority and the Section 29 parties are notified about the Secretary of State's views and may submit written observations. If, however, the Secretary of State receives a new evidence or intends to base his decision on new fact not raised at the inquiry, he must notify the parties, who are entitled to make representations within 21 days and then the Secretary of State has to re-open the inquiry. When the Secretary of State decides the case, he usually sends a copy of the Inspector's report to the parties, and he must do so if either party requests it.

Inquiries in respect of development plans are somewhat different. These are inquiries into the objection to the plan and not into the plan as a whole. In this case it is usually the local planning authority who opens the case. Then the objectors present their objections.

The Secretary of State is not obliged to give reason for his decision in respect of the development plans, but he has to do so on the request of interested parties.

Chapter 10

ACQUISITION OF LAND

General

The Town and Country Planning Act 1968 granted wide powers to the local planning authorities for the compulsory acquisition of land for development and other planning purposes. These provisions are now consolidated in Part VI of the Town and Country Planning Act 1971 (Sections 112-133).

The Secretary of State may authorise a local authority (not necessarily a local planning authority) to acquire land compulsorily within its area if he is satisfied;

(a) that the land is required in order to secure the treatment as a whole, by development, or redevelopment, or improvement, of the land; or

(b) that it is expedient in the public interest that the land should be held with the land so required; or

(c) that the land is required for the purpose of providing for the relocation of population or industry or the replacement of open space in the course of redevelopment or improvement; or

(d) that it is expedient to acquire the land immediately for a purpose which it is necessary to achieve in the interest of the proper planning of an area in which the land is situated.

The Secretary of State, after consulting with the interested authorities may also authorise the acquisition of land situated within the area of another local authority.

The local authorities which may be authorised to purchase land compulsorily are County Counties, County Boroughs and County Districts (in London both the Greater London Council and Councils of London Boroughs).

In addition the Secretary of State for the Environment may acquire compulsorily any land necessary for public purposes, or acquire an easement or other right over land.

These powers of compulsory purchase are very far reaching and it

70

is expected that the 1971 Act will be used extensively instead of the many other Acts granting power to acquire land compulsorily.

Listed Buildings

Sections 114-117 contain special provisions in respect of acquisition of listed buildings, i.e. buildings having a special historical or architectural interest.

If such a building is not properly maintained, the Secretary of State may himself compulsorily acquire the land, or authorise the local planning authority to take this action. Before, however, a compulsory purchase order is issued, a notice must be sent to the owner, specifying the works which are considered reasonably necessary for the proper preservation of the building and explaining the Secretary of State's or the local authority's power of compulsory purchase.

Only if the notice is not complied with within two months, may acquisition be effected.

Any person having an interest in the listed building which is subject to a compulsory purchase order may apply to the Magistrate's Court for an order staying further proceedings on the compulsory purchase order, and if the Court is satisfied that reasonable steps have been taken for the preservation of the building, the Court may make an order accordingly. An appeal is allowed to the Crown Court against the decision of the Magistrates' Court.

'Minimum Compensation' in Respect of Listed Buildings

If it has been established that the building has been allowed to fall into disrepair deliberately for the purpose of justifying the redevelopment of the site, the compulsory purchase order may include a direction that the assessment of compensation shall be subject to 'minimum compensation'. This means that the compensation will be the price which disregards any profit which may have accrued from the redevelopment of the site. There is a right of appeal against a direction for minimum compensation to the Magistrate's Court with a further appeal to the Crown Court.

Additional Powers in Respect of Land Compulsorily Acquired

Under Section 30 of the 1968 Act (not repealed by the 1971 Act) the acquiring authority, after obtaining a valid compulsory purchase order, may obtain actual ownership of the whole interest in land by executing a 'general vesting declaration'. Such a declaration can be made not earlier than two months after the compulsory purchase has been confirmed. The notice informing the parties that the compulsory purchase order has been confirmed must contain a statement about the powers of the local authority to execute a general vesting declaration and about the right of the parties to claim compensation. The general vesting declaration must be served by the local authority on every occupier of the land and on every person who has indicated an intention to claim compensation for the land compulsorily acquired. The detailed provisions concerning this way of acquisition are contained in Schedule 3 to the 1968 Act (not repealed) and in the Compulsory Purchase of Land (General Vesting Declaration) Regulations 1969 (S.I. No. 425).

Acquisition of Land by Agreement

The council of any County, County Borough (until 31 March 1974 when the County Boroughs will disappear) or County District may acquire by agreement:

(a) any land which they require for any purpose for which a local authority may be authorised to acquire land compulsorily under Section 112 of the Act; or

(b) any building appearing to them to be of special architectural or historical interest; or

(c) any building comprising or contiguous or adjacent to such a building which appears to the Secretary of State to be required for preserving the buildings or its amenities or for affording access to it or for its proper control of management.

Land may also be acquired for the purpose of exchanging it for land required for planning purposes or for the green belt around London.

The consent of the Secretary of State is required unless the land is immediately required by the council for the purpose for which it is to be acquired, or is land within the area of the council acquiring the land. Thus, in effect, permission of the Secretary of State will seldom be required.

Where a local authority has acquired land for planning purposes they may, instead of developing it themselves, dispose of it to such person, in such manner and subject to such conditions, as may appear to them to be expedient.

72

Sometimes the consent of the Secretary of State is required, namely for any disposal:

(a) by an authority other than County, County Borough or County District; or

(b) of land acquired for planning purposes in connection with development, redevelopment or improvement; or

(c) of land which is part of a common.

Thus the land may be disposed (i.e. sold or leased) to a developer who has no powers of compulsory purchase, but who is prepared to develop the land. Much land after the war has been developed in this manner. The Secretary of State may require a local planning authority to dispose of it to a specified person, but only for the best price reasonably obtainable.

Such disposal has to secure, as far as practicable, that persons formerly living or carrying on business on such land may be able to get accommodation on the land at a suitable price.

Agreements Regulating Development or Use of Land

A local planning authority may enter into an agreement with any person interested in land in their area for the purpose of restricting or regulating the development of land either permanently or during such period as may be prescribed by the agreement. Any such agreement may contain such incidental and consequential provisions (including the provisions of a financial character) as appear to the local authority to be necessary or expedient for the purpose of the agreement. (Section 119).

Since 1968 it has not been necessary to obtain the Secretary of State's approval for such an agreement, which was required under previous Acts.

Such an agreement may be enforced against the developer and his successor in title like any other restrictive covenant. Section 52(2) states that the agreement may be enforced by the local planning authority against persons deriving titles, as if the local authority were possessed of adjacent land and as if the agreement had been expressed to be made for the benefit of such land. It continues: nothing in the agreement shall be construed as restricting any power exercisable by any Minister or local authority under the Act as long as those powers are exercised in accordance with the provisions of the development plan. Thus, although it enables the Secretary of State or the local authority to override the agreement, nevertheless it is a considerable restriction of their powers, as otherwise they would be able to override the agreement without any qualification. If the agreement is broken, presumably compensation is payable, as it would be an interference with a development lawfully executed. The agreement may also be entered into by a district council in respect of land within its area.

In some of these cases it seems that the planning permission is granted as part of a bargain under which the landowner voluntarily accepts conditions, which would be quashed by the Court if imposed on the granting of planning permission.

In practice, the total number of agreements has been small. For example, in the four years' period between 1956-1959 there were only 83 agreements concluded.[1]

One of the more publicised agreements between a local authority and a developer, was that between the Oldham Estates Company Limited and the London County Council for the development of St Giles Circus. The London County Council was anxious to improve traffic flow in an area where Oldham Estates already had substantial freehold interests and were proposing to acquire further land and redevelop the whole area. Rather than work in opposition to each other, it would appear that an agreement was made whereby Oldham Estates acquired the land required by the London County Council for their road scheme and dedicated it to them. In exchange the London County Council granted planning permission for Oldham Estates development on the site they retained with floor space appropriate to the total area. The ultimate development, 'Centre Point', has been the subject of much press and political comment.

Procedure of Compulsory Purchase of Land for Planning Purposes

The Acquisition of Land (Authorisation Procedure) Act 1946, the Compulsory Purchase Act 1965 and the Land Compensation Act 1961 govern the procedure for the acquisition of land for planning purposes with a few minor amendments.

Chapter 11

COMPENSATION FOR PLANNING DECISIONS

Introduction

Planning control, as explained in the previous chapters, creates a problem arising from the fact that planning decisions very often result in losses for the owner of the land.

If land is compulsorily purchased, i.e. if the owner is deprived of the property in the land, the principle is that property shall not be compulsorily acquired without full compensation. This principle was judicially recognised in the leading case of Attorney General v. De Keyser's Royal Hotel Ltd. (1920 A.C. 508), where it was said: 'it is a well established principle that unless no other interpretation is possible, justice requires that statutes should not be construed to enable the land of a particular individual to be confiscated without payment'. There is no legislation in the present system of the English law which enables the government to confiscate property without compensation assessed according to existing rules.

On the other hand, there is another general principle that compensation is not payable for any restrictions in the use of the property, unless an Act of Parliament expressly so provides. In many instances (in Public Health Acts, Landlord and Tenant or Rent Acts and Housing Acts) use of the land by the owner is restricted without any compensation.

But, as decisions under the Town and County Planning Acts restrict the use of land much more than other legislation, they amount to some partial confiscation, if not of the property itself, then, at least, of some rights of use over it. It is recognised that many planning restrictions are in effect confiscatory and for this reason compensation is provided by legislation in respect of some planning restrictions.

Two parts of the 1971 Act deal with compensation for planning restrictions. Part VII deals with compensation for planning decisions restricting 'new development'; Part VIII with compensation for other planning restrictions.

Section 22, after giving the general definition of development, divided it into 'development' (usually called 'existing use development') and 'new development'; 'new development' being any development other than a development specified in Part I or Part II of the Schedule 8 to the Act.

In order to explain the reasons for dividing development into these two categories, it is necessary to consider the Government's policy behind the 1947 Town and Country Planning Act, which for the first time, created this distinction.

The Act of 1947 did not nationalise land itself as considered by the Uthwatt Report[1] in order to ensure adequate control of development, but (without using this expression) virtually nationalised development rights in the land. The Government nationalised only future development rights, i.e. development rights which would accrue after the 1947 Act came into operation, i.e. after 1 July 1948.

Since it was realised that it might be difficult to decide which development value accrued after 1 July 1948 (and, therefore, belongs to the State) and which accrued before that date (and so had not been expropriated), it was decided to 'nationalise' all development values, whether existing on 1 July 1948, or accruing later, and to pay compensation for rights existing on 1 July 1948. A sum of £300 million was earmarked as compensation for the rights existing on 1 July 1948 (mostly 'suburban' land) and the owners of such land were invited to submit claims within 12 months. The claims submitted amounted to more than £300 million and, after allocating the full amounts claimed to some 'near ripe' developments, the balance was allocated to other claims, which were met almost in full (80 new pence for each Pound claimed). The money itself was not paid, but the claims were noted in a special register. It was originally intended to pay the claims within seven years, but this intention was abandoned in 1953, and these claims are now known (after some adjustments) as 'unexpended balance of established development value'.

Developments enumerated in Schedule 8 to the 1971 Act (previously Schedule 3 to the 1947 and 1962 Acts, hence called 'Schedule Three Developments'), were exempted from the 'nationalisation' scheme. They were developments consistent with, or required for, the existing use of land or building in question. As no claims were allowed in respect of these developments, the deprivation of compensation for refusal of these developments amounts to confiscation without compensation.

Although the 'unexpended balance of the established development value' was not paid, the claims for this balance are outstanding and are used as a limit of compensation for planning decisions restricting 'new' development.

Consequently, the value of the existing use developments is treated differently from the value of the new development as regards compensation for restricting planning decisions.

Chapter 12

COMPENSATION FOR PLANNING DECISIONS RESTRICTING NEW DEVELOPMENT

Part VI of the Act deals with compensation in respect of 'new development', i.e. development outside the scope of Schedule 8.

In order to obtain compensation if planning permission is refused or is granted subject to conditions, it must be shown in the first instance that the land in question has an unexpended balance of established development value.

Any compensation paid under this part of the Act will be deducted from the unexpended balance, and if the compensation due exceeds the amount of the unexpended balance, only the balance will be paid. This means that compensation amounts either to the depreciation of the value in the land due to refusal or to the condition attached to the decision of the local planning authority, or to the unexpended balance, whichever is the less.

Consequently, if development is allowed at a later date, then the compensation paid to the owner has to repaid.

However, some planning decisions do not rank for compensation, even if there is an unexpended balance attached to the land (Section 147).

Compensation shall not be payable:

(a) in respect of the refusal of planning permission for any development which consists of or includes the making of any material change in the use of any building or other land.

As the majority of applications for planning permission in built-up areas are for changes of use, it follows that compensation will not often be payable in connection with applications for such developments.

The reason for this exclusion seems to be that although the intended change of use might enhance the value of the land, nevertheless the existing use of the land established for many years has, apparently, not been injurious to the developer, as otherwise he would not have kept the land in the existing use for years.

(b) on the refusal of planning permission for the display of advertisements or on the grant of it subject to conditions. Apparently, as the advertisement may be offensive to the environment, the Government wants to retain the right to refuse permission in this respect without being called upon to pay compensation.

(c) on imposing conditions relating to:

— the number or disposition of buildings on any land;

— the dimensions, design, structure or external appearance of any building, or the materials to be used in its construction;

— the manner in which any land is to be laid out for the purposes of development, including the provisions for parking, loading, unloading, or fuelling of vehicles on the land;

— the use of any building or other land;

— the location or design of any means of access to a highway, or the material to be used in the construction.

Thus the Government reserves for itself a free hand in respect of the matters mentioned above and is not obliged to pay compensation for imposing conditions pertaining to them.

(d) on imposing conditions on the duration of planning permission (Section 41), reserved matters in outline planning permission (Section 42), or conditions imposed by the Industrial Development Certificate (Section 71) or Office Development Permit (Section 82);

(e) if the reason for the refusal is that the development will be premature due to:

— the order of priority indicated in the development plan for the area in which the land is situated, for the development in that area;

— any existing deficiency in the provision of water supplies or sewerage services, and the period within which any such deficiency may reasonably be expected to be made good;

However, in the case of premature application, delay in providing the services cannot be longer than seven years, and if the applicant makes another application after the expiration of seven years and the permission is still considered premature, compensation will be paid.

(f) if the reason for the refusal is that the land is unsuitable

79

for the proposed development because of its liability to flooding or subsidence;

It may be assumed that such applications may be made in bad faith and only in order to obtain compensation after the expected refusal.

(g) if, notwithstanding the refusal, permission for an alternative development may be granted. This provision applies to any development of a residential, commercial or industrial character, being a development which consists wholly or mainly of the construction of houses, flats, shops or office premises, or industrial buildings (Section 148);

The reason for this provision is that, provided some reasonable remunerative development is allowed, the owner is not entitled to compensation only because he envisages the most profitable development.

(h) if the Secretary of State issues a direction under Section 38. This Section allows the Secretary of State to review the planning decision issued by the local planning authority, which would involve the payment of compensation, in such a manner as to avoid the payment of compensation and vary it in favour of the applicant.

Before the Secretary of State interferes with the decision of the local authority he must give notice to the applicant and to the local authority and, on request of either of them, must afford each an opportunity to be heard by an Inspector.

If the owner, who intends to apply for permission for development, is unable to obtain an Industrial Development Certificate, he may nevertheless claim compensation if he can obtain a notice under Section 72 of the Act, which is issued by the local planning authority and states that the local authority would refuse permission even if a formal application, supported by an Industrial Development Certificate would be submitted to them (Section 151).

If, however, the owner is unable to obtain an Office Development Permit, he is left without remedy.

Claims for compensation under Part VII of the Act must be submitted within six months of the relevant decision and must be sent to the local planning authority for transmission to the Secretary of State, together with any evidence and information provided by the claimant and considered relevant by the authority or the Secretary of State. If it appears to the Secretary of State that the claim is not justified, he has to notify the claimant and invite him to withdraw the claim. If the claim is not withdrawn, the Secretary of State gives notice to all persons having interests in the land (Section 154).

Questions as to whether the claim is justified, what should be the amount of claim, and how it should be apportioned are decided in disputed cases by the Lands Tribunal (Section 156).

Chapter 13

COMPENSATION FOR OTHER PLANNING RESTRICTIONS

General

Compensation is also due for a variety of other planning restrictions, which impose undue loss on the claimant.

They are dealt with in Part VIII of the Act under the following headings:

(a) compensation for the revocation or modification of planning permission;

(b) compensation for planning decisions restricting development other than new developments (as the latter are dealt with in Part VII of the Act);

(c) compensation in respect of orders under Section 51, requiring the discontinuance of the use or the alteration or the removal of buildings or works;

(d) compensation for the refusal to consent to the alteration, etc. of listed building;

(e) compensation where listed building consent is revoked or modified;

(f) compensation for loss or damage caused by the serving of a building preservation notice;

(g) compensation in respect of a Tree Preservation Order;

(h) compensation in respect of requirements as to replanting of trees;

(i) compensation for restriction on advertising;

(j) compensation for loss due to a stop notice.

Compensation for Revocation or Modification of Planning Permission (Sections 164-168)

Under Section 45 (see Chapter 5) the local planning authority may revoke or modify permission to develop land at any time before the operation in question has been completed or a change of use has taken place. Unopposed revocation or modification may be exercised by the local planning authority itself, but if it is opposed by the claimant it requires confirmation by the Secretary of State.

If the order was opposed and confirmed by the Secretary of State, compensation is payable by the local planning authority for expenditure in carrying out work which has been rendered abortive by the revocation or modification or for loss which is directly attributable to the revocation or modification. Preparatory work (e.g. the drawing of plans) may be included in the claim. Even if the permission in question, which has been revoked or modified had been granted not by express permission of the local planning authority but by the General Development Order, compensation may be claimed.

The Town and Country Planning General Regulations 1969 (S.I. No. 286) prescribe the detailed procedure in respect of claiming compensation. Compensation must be claimed from the local planning authority within six months. Any compensation exceeding £20 is apportioned between the various parts of the land and registered as a local land charge, as it will be recoverable by the local authority on subsequent permission to carry on development.

Compensation for Planning Decisions Restricting Development other than New Development (Section 169)

'Existing use developments' (i.e. developments which are other than 'new developments') are listed in Schedule 8 (in the 1947 and 1962 Acts they were listed in Schedule 3 to those Acts, hence they are often called 'Schedule Three Developments').

The Schedule specifies eight classes of development, some involving operations, some changes of use.

The Schedule does not give permission for any of those forms of development, but it has some bearing on the rights of the owner, as in the compulsory acquisition of land the compensation given assumes that planning permission would be granted for any class of development specified in the Schedule 8.

The Schedule divides the 'existing use developments' into two categories. Part I of the Schedule describes developments which do not rank for compensation under Section 160 for refusal of permission to carry them out. Part II describes developments which do rank for compensation on the refusal of permission.

The following developments, given in Part I, do not rank for compensation:

The carrying out of any of the following works:

(a) the rebuilding of any building existing on 1st July 1948, or any building destroyed or demolished between 7 January 1937 and 1 July 1948, or any building in existence at a 'material date', i.e. at the date of the relevant planning decision (this means the date of the decision which may give the right to compensation). The rebuilding includes the making good of any war damage;

(b) the carrying out of works for the maintenance, improvement or other alteration of any building, being work which affects only the interior of the building or which does not materially affect its external appearance and is work for making good war damage;

In both the above cases the cubic content of the original building should not exceed:

— in the case of a dwelling house, more than one-tenth of the volume or 1750 cubic feet, whichever is greater, and

— in any other case by more than one-tenth of the volume of the building.

(c) the conversion of any building which on 1 July 1948 was used as a single dwelling house into two or more separate dwellings.

Part I of the Schedule does not create any problem in relation to compensation for refusal of permission to develop, as these developments do not rank for compensation. The reason is that in war-damaged buildings war damage is paid and if the development is not permitted, the owner can serve a purchase notice on the local authority asking it to buy the land if it is not capable of reasonable beneficial use. In other buildings that have been destroyed it is assumed that insurance was paid and again the claimant has not suffered loss. In all these cases it may be in the interest of the community that the buildings should not necessarily be rebuilt in the same manner as they previously existed. Some other development may be more suitable.

Part II of the Schedule 8 lists six developments (some of them being operations, some of them changes of use) which do rank for compensation if permission in respect of them is refused:

(a) the enlargement, improvement or other alteration of any building which is in any of the categories listed above under point (b), if the enlargement is within the limits given in Part I of the Schedule (i.e. one-tenth of the cubic content);

The original wording was amended in 1963 by providing that

84

not only the cubic space, but also the floor space should not be exceeded by more than 10%. The reason for this condition was that in alteration of a building, by lowering the ceiling height it is possible to extend the useful floor space extensively up to 40%, but still keeping the increase of cubic content within 10%.

(b) the carrying out on land used for agriculture or forestry of any building or other operations required for that use. The erection, enlargement or improvement of the following buildings are excluded:

— dwelling houses;

— buildings used as market gardens;

— buildings used for purposes not connected with farming or forestry operations.

(c) the winning and working on land held for agricultural purposes of any minerals required for that use;

(d) any change of use within the Use Classes Order.

It should be mentioned that the 'Use Classes Order for the Purpose of the Third Schedule' was originally identical to the 'Use Classes Order' for the purpose of defining permitted development, but now there are small differences and when there are differences there is a necessity for applying for permission and, on refusal, a possibility of claiming compensation. When the terms are identical, no permission for development is necessary and the question of compensation does not arise.

Any interference with development permitted under the Use Classes Order, of course, attracts compensation.

(e) where only a part of a building erected before 1 July 1948 or other land is used for a particular purpose, the use for that purpose of an additional part not exceeding one-tenth of the part used for that purpose;

(f) the deposit of waste materials or refuse in connection with mineral working on a site used for that purpose.

The conditions for obtaining compensation for the refusal of permission in respect of Schedule 8 (Part II) developments, may be summarised as follows:

(a) the development must, of course, fall within Part II of the 8th Schedule;

(b) planning permission must have been refused by the Secretary of State, which means that if the decision is taken by a local planning authority, an appeal to the Secretary of State is imperative.

85

(c) there must be a diminution in the value of the interest as a result of the Secretary of State's decision;

(d) the claim must be submitted within six months to the local authority. This period may be extended by the Secretary of State.

Compensation in Respect of Order under Section 51 (i.e. Order Requiring Discontinuance of Use or Alteration or Removal of Buildings or Works) (Section 170)

The proper planning of land may, from time to time, require the removal of a building or the prohibition of use undertaken with due planning permission. Such orders, under Section 51, entitle any person suffering loss to apply for compensation. The compensation is equivalent to the depreciation of the value in the land and expenses reasonably incurred in carrying out any works in compliance with the order.

Compensation in respect of Listed Buildings (Sections 171-172)

There are three types of compensation in respect of listed buildings:

The first type of compensation is due if an application for consent to alter a listed building is refused, and such an alteration does not constitute a development or is a development allowed by the General Development Order. In such circumstances it is clear that the owner suffers loss for the sole reason that the building is listed, because otherwise he would be able to carry out the work. A condition of this type of compensation is that the application must be refused by the Secretary of State, and not only by the local authority; thus the applicant, if the refusal is given by the local planning authority must, in the first instance, appeal against the decision. The extent of compensation is the amount by which the value of the building has been notionally reduced by the refusal of the alteration or extension.

The second type of compensation in respect of listed buildings is due where the listed building consent has been revoked or modified. If a person has incurred expenditure in carrying out works which were rendered abortive or has otherwise sustained loss or damage which is directly attributable to the revocation or modification, the authority has to pay compensation in respect of that expenditure, loss or damage.

The third type of compensation refers to the loss or damage attributable directly to the issue of a Building Preservation Notice. If the building to which a Building Preservation Notice refers has not in fact been listed, the Building Preservation Notice eventually ceases to have effect. Compensation is then due to cover the expenditure, damage or loss sustained by the fact that the abortive Building Preservation Notice had been served.

Compensation in Respect of Tree Preservation (Sections 174-175)

Compensation is due in respect of loss or damage caused in consequence of the refusal of any consent required under the Tree Preservation Order, or if consent is granted subject to conditions.

If in pursuance of provisions made by the Tree Preservation Order, a direction is given for securing the replanting of trees, which have been felled in the course of an operation permitted under the order, compensation is due. The compensation is conditional on a certificate of the Forestry Commission that they will not pay a grant, which may be due under Section 4 of the Forestry Act 1967. This condition is imposed in order to avoid the payment of double compensation.

Compensation for Restriction of Advertisements (Section 176)

If a person is compelled to remove an advertisement which has been displayed since 1 August 1948, or to discontinue the use of a site for the purposes of advertising which was so used on that date, he is entitled to recover compensation in respect of any expenses reasonably incurred by him on that behalf, as before 1 August 1948 no permission was required for displaying advertisements.

Compensation for Loss due to Stop Notice (Section 177)

Where a Stop Notice issued under Section 90 of the Act ceases to have effect a person who at the time when it was served had an interest in the land may be entitled to compensation.

It will remembered that the Stop Notice's validity depends on the existence of the enforcement notice. If, therefore, the enforcement notice is quashed on appeal or is withdrawn, then the Stop Notice also ceases to have effect. Appeals against enforcement notices can be made on seven specified grounds which have been explained in Chapter 8. The grounds of appeal in paragraphs (b) to (e) allege fault on the part of the local authority, because in these four cases the enforcement notice should not have been issued by the local authority in the first place. But if appeals succeed on the grounds enumerated under (a), (f) and (g), it is not because the enforcement notice should not have been issued, but because a discretionary consideration has additionally been given to the problem and it has been decided to take a more lenient view of the breach. In those latter cases, however, the local planning authority was fully justified in issuing an enforcement notice.

For these reasons in the following circumstances compensation is payable for loss attributable to Stop Notice:

(a) if the enforcement notice has been quashed on the grounds mentioned in Section 88(1) paragraphs (b), (c), (d) or (e);

(b) if the allegation in the enforcement notice on which the prohibition in the Stop Notice is dependent is not upheld by reason that the enforcement notice has been varied on one of those grounds;

(c) if the enforcement notice is withdrawn (otherwise than as a result of the granting of belated planning permission);

(d) if the stop notice itself is withdrawn.

An application for compensation should be submitted to the local planning authority within six months.

Compensation is payable only to a person having an interest in the land, so that a contractor who complies with a Stop Notice served on him has no direct claim against the local authority, but can claim damages from his employer for breach of contract. The employer can include in his claim damages paid to the contractor for the breach of contract. Where the contract was made before 1 January 1970, the employer is deemed to be in breach of contract (Section 90(8)), unless the contract makes provisions explicitly to the contrary. In contracts made after that date the presumption does not operate and the rights of the contractor in this respect should be clearly stated in the contract between him and the employer.

Generally the compensation is assessed under the provisions of the Land Compensation Act 1961 and the amount of compensation, in case of a dispute is assessed by the Land Tribunal.

Generally speaking claims for payment of compensation should be made to and paid by the local planning authority which took the action by virtue of which the claim arose. There are some detailed provisions in this respect in Paragraphs 34-36 of the 16th Schedule to the Local Government Act 1972.

Chapter 14

PURCHASE NOTICE BY
OWNERS — PLANNING BLIGHT

General

Many planning decisions do not allow the owner to use land in the most profitable manner and, as has been seen, he can, under certain circumstances, obtain compensation for his loss.

In some cases, however, the land, because of planning restrictions, is of no value to the owner, or, in the words of the statute, 'is not capable of reasonably beneficial use'. In these circumstances it is equitable that the owner should have the right to ask the local authority to purchase his interest in the land, which has lost its value to him. The second situation, in which the owner of an interest in land may be severely injured, occurs when the development plan 'blights' some areas, i.e. allocates them in such a manner as to depreciate the value of the land. In this situation it is also equitable that the local authority under some conditions should be obliged to acquire the land.

Thus a purchase notice may be served by the owner in some cases of:

    (a) adverse planning decisions;

    (b) adverse planning proposals (so called 'planning blight').

Interests Affected by Planning Decisions and Orders (Sections 180-191)

If an application for planning permission is refused or granted subject to conditions, and the owner of the interest in land claims:

    (a) that the land has become incapable of reasonably beneficial use in the existing state, *and*

    (b) in a case where the planning permission was granted subject to conditions, that the land cannot be rendered capable of reasonably beneficial use by carrying out the permitted development subject to those conditions, *and*

89

(c) in any case that the land cannot be rendered capable of reasonably beneficial use by the carrying out of any other development for which planning permission has been granted, or for which the local planning authority or the Secretary of State has undertaken to grant planning permission,

then he may, within six months, serve on the local authority a notice requiring that authority to purchase his interest in the land in question.

In determining what would be a reasonably beneficial use no account is to be taken of the possibility of any 'new development' (i.e. outside the scope of Schedule 8). Thus, it is not open to the owner to show that the existing use of land is substantially less profitable than it would have been if a new development were permitted. In addition the 'purchase notice' cannot be served if the intended development would contravene the conditions set out in Schedule 18. This means that the intended re-building or re-using of the building cannot entail an extension by more than 10% of the *floor* space of the building, and not only an extension of the volume, as under Schedule 8 (which defines existing use development). This additional limitation was introduced because by lowering the height of the ceiling it was possible to increase the floor space up to 40%, keeping the increase of volume within the permitted limits of 10%.

The fact, however, that no Industrial Development Certificate, or Office Development Permit has been refused does not affect the possibility of a claim.

The local authority on which the owner has served the purchase notice can comply with the notice and agree to buy the land in question, or can find another local authority or statutory undertaker which is willing to acquire the land, but if neither of these eventualities can materialise, must submit the purchase notice to the Secretary of State, who has to approve it before it becomes operative.

The Secretary of State may either confirm the purchase notice or he may grant permission for the development sought by the owner, or he may grant permission for some other kind of development, which would render the land capable of reasonably beneficial use. The Secretary of State must give notice to persons affected by his proposed action and the persons concerned must be given an opportunity of being heard by the Inspector.

It frequently happens that when an application is made for

planning permission to develop a small housing estate, some open space or 'amenity land' is left out, or sometimes the authority imposes a condition requiring the preservation of the 'amenity land'. According to the court decision in the case of Adams and Wade v. Minister of Housing and Local Government and Workington Rural District Council (*Estate Gazette*, 1965, page 649), a developer could submit a further application for the development of the open space and, on receiving the expected refusal of permission, successfully require the local authority to purchase it under a purchase notice at housing value.

Section 184, however, enables the Secretary of State to refuse to confirm the purchase notice if he is satisfied that the land ought to remain as 'amenity land' for the benefit of the development authorised in the earlier permission.

The Secretary of State's decision, whether to confirm the purchase notice or to refuse to confirm it, or to grant permission for other development, may be challenged in the High Court on a point of law within six weeks.

If the Secretary of State does not issue any decision:

(a) within nine months of the service of the purchase notice by the owner;

(b) within six months of the submission of the copy of the purchase notice to the Secretary of State (whichever period expires earlier); the notice shall be deemed to have been confirmed.

A purchase notice may be served by the owner not only if permission to develop the land is refused, but also on the revocation or modification of planning permission, or if the local planning authority issues an order requiring the discontinuance of use or alteration or removal of building or works. A purchase notice can also be served if a listed building consent is refused, if consent in respect of a Tree Preservation Order is refused, or if permission to display advertisements is denied.

The conditions and procedure for the service of purchase notices in these special cases are broadly similar to those in respect of refusal of planning permission in those cases.

Interests of Owner-occupiers Affected by the Planning Proposals ('Planning Blight'). Sections 192-207

In some cases planning proposals affect the interest of the

owner-occupier to such an extent that it is equitable to enable him to serve a purchase notice which is called 'blight notice' in the Act.

Section 192 enumerates ten circumstances in which a 'blight notice' may be served. They may be summarised as follows:

(a) the land is indicated in a structure or local plan as required by a government department, local government, statutory undertakers or the National Coal Board, or is included in an action area; or

(b) it is land on which a highway is proposed to be constructed; or

(c) it is land included in the general improvement area under Section 31 of the Housing Act 1969; or

(d) it is land in respect of which a compulsory purchase order is in force, but notice to treat has not yet been served. (This means that the authority in question have acquired power to purchase the land compulsorily, but have not yet undertaken any steps to exercise the power).

Thus a 'blight notice' refers exclusively to the cases where the land may be compulsorily purchased in the future. The need for the notice is the fact that the project affects the price of the land and may even make it unsaleable.

The blight notice may be served by a resident owner-occupier of a dwelling house irrespective of its annual value, but an owner-occupier of any other type of land (i.e. not being a dwelling house) can serve a blight notice only if the annual value of the hereditament in question does not exceed £750. There is a special consideration for the owner-occupier of agricultural units, as he is entitled to serve a blight notice irrespective of annual value of the unit if his land is wholly or even partially contained in blighted area. The term owner-occupier includes a freeholder or a leaseholder with at least three years to run; also, in addition, a mortgagee, if affected by the blight (as his security may be diminished), may serve a blight notice.

A person who intends to serve a blight notice must claim that:

(a) he is entitled to an interest in that hereditament or unit;

(b) the interest is one which qualifies for protection under the provisions of the Act;

(c) since the relevant date, he has made reasonable endeavours to sell that interest;

(d) he has been unable to sell it, except at a price substantially lower than that for which he may reasonably have expected to sell, if no part of the hereditament or unit was blighted.

The blight notice has to be served in respect of the whole land blighted or in respect of the whole part of the land which is affected by the blight.

The local authority may within two months after receiving the blight notice serve on the claimant an objection to the notice. The objection must be based on one of the eight grounds specified in Section 194. Generally speaking an objection may be based on the fact that the conditions of serving the notice are not satisfied. One reason for objecting is worthy of attention: if the land is blighted due to its inclusion for a specified purpose in a development plan, the local authority may base its objection on the issuing of a certificate that the land will not be required in the course of the next 15 years. When a notice of objection has been served, the owner-occupier may, within two months, require the matter to be referred for a decision of the Land Tribunal. The onus to prove that the notice of objection is not well founded is on the owner-occupier.

If the local authority does not serve a notice of objection, or if it is not upheld by the Land Tribunal, the local authority is deemed to be authorised to acquire the land in question, and to have served a notice to treat. Thus the local authority is not only authorised, but also obliged to acquire the land.

The compensation is the price of the land in an 'unblighted' condition and may include compensation for disturbance and injurious affection (see Part II of the book).

It is the district planning authority which pays compensation when purchase notice has been served by the owner of the land.

Chapter 15

HIGHWAYS

A highway is defined as land over which the public at large has a right of pass and re-pass. Although the common law rule is 'once a highway, always a highway', a number of Acts, and in particular the Town and Country Planning Act 1971, give the authorities large powers in respect of highways. (Sections 209-221.)

The Secretary of State may by order authorise the stopping up or diversion of any highway, if he is satisfied that it is necessary to do so in order to enable the development to be carried out in accordance with planning permission, or to be carried out by a government department.

Footpath and bridleways may be stopped or diverted by the 'competent authority', that is the local planning authority, or the authority to which planning authority delegated its powers.

A highway, which is not a trunk or special road, may be converted into a footpath or a bridleway by an order issued by the Secretary of State. If, due to the issue of such an order, somebody's land depreciates in value by the deprivation of access to a road, the person affected may claim compensation.

The Secretary of State may by order extinguish a public right of way over land being subject to development, provided that he is satisfied that an alternative right of way is, or will be, provided.

The Secretary of State or a local planning authority may be authorised to acquire land compulsorily, for the purposes of providing or improving any highway or for providing any right of way, if it is done for the purpose of realising planning proposals.

The Act provides detailed procedure for putting these orders into effect.

Chapter 16

TOWN AND COUNTRY PLANNING LAW FOR GREATER LONDON

The special provisions of the town and country planning law for Greater London are contained in:

(a) Schedule 3 to the Town and Country Planning Act 1971 which designates local planning authorities for Greater London;

(b) Schedule 1 to the Town and Country Planning (Amendment) Act 1972, which replaced Schedule 4 to the Town and Country Planning Act 1971 and deals with surveys and development plans for Greater London;

(c) Part II of Schedule 5 to the Town and Country Planning Act 1971 which contains transitory provisions for Greater London due to the existence of old and new styles of the development plans;

(d) Paragraph 39 of the Schedule 16 to the Local Government Act 1972 which deals with stopping up and diversion of highways;

(e) Town and Country Planning (Local Planning Authorities in Greater London) Regulations 1965 S.I.No.679, as amended by the Town and Country Planning (Local Planning Authorities in Greater London) (Amendment) Regulations 1967 S.I.No.430;

(f) Town and Country Planning (Development Order for Greater London) Regulations 1966 S.I.No.48, as amended by the Town and Country Planning (Development Plan for Greater London) (Amendment) Regulations 1968 S.I.No.815.

The Greater London Council is the local planning authority for Greater London as a whole, but within certain limits the individual councils of the London Boroughs are the local planning authorities for certain planning purposes within those Boroughs. The most important provisions, which are peculiar to Greater London are outlined in this chapter.

Surveys and Development Plans

Surveys should be prepared by both the Greater London Council and by London Borough Councils. The Greater London Council is not required to cover all matters which, according to Section 6 of the 1971 Act should be dealt with in the survey, but should cover only such matters as they think fit, or as may be specified by the Secretary of State.

London Boroughs should prepare the surveys and keep under review those matters, mentioned in Section 6 of the Act, which have not been examined by the Greater London Council, such other matters as may be required by that Council to examine, or such matters as may be specified by a direction issued by the Secretary of State.

Any two or more London Borough councils may institute a joint survey for any combined area consisting of those boroughs or any parts thereof.

The Greater London Development Plan (which had been originally prepared in draft under the 'old style' procedure) shall be a structure plan for Greater London approved under Section 9 of the Town and Country Planning Act 1971 and may be altered under the general provisions of that Act. With respect to Greater London its structure plan may be approved by the Secretary of State by stages, so that he may approve any feature or element of the plan, reserving his decisions as to the remaining part. Thus, for instance, early approval may be granted for the development of Covent Garden, dockland or the extension of the London Transport underground system.

In Greater London there may be two types of local plans. If the Greater London development plan indicates an area as a 'Greater London Council action area', the local plan for that area is prepared by the Greater London Council. Otherwise any London Borough council may prepare a local plan for the whole or any part of the Borough, but, of course, with the exclusion of a Greater London Council action area. Two or more London Boroughs may prepare a joint local plan.

It is the duty of the Greater London Council to prepare local plans for their action area, and it is the duty of any London Borough council to prepare local plans for other action areas.

The procedure governing the preparation of the local plans (either by the Greater London Council or by the London Borough

96

councils) differs from the procedure prescribed for the rest of the country.

The local plan shall consist of a map and a written statement, formulating the proposals for development, or other use of the land in the area and indicating the measures for the improvement of the physical environment, the management of traffic, and other matters prescribed by the Secretary of State.

All local plans must conform generally to the Greater London development plan and the Secretary of State on receiving information that formalities in respect of publicity for the preparation of a local plan or in respect of the opportunity of making representations have not been preserved, can suspend the adoption of the local plan.

Control of Development

The control of development is divided between the Greater London Council and London Boroughs. The division of responsibilities can be given in outline only, since it is provided that many details will be clarified by statutory instruments which may modify the responsibility of the Greater London Planning authorities.

London Boroughs will deal with any planning application under Part III of the 1971 Act, i.e. with any application for permission for development which is subject to general planning control. With respect to control in special cases, only applications for listed building consent are within the jurisdiction of the London Boroughs, and applications in respect of all other special cases (trees, advertisements, waste land, industrial development and office development) are to be dealt with by the Greater London Council. Usually (except in any case or class of cases in respect of which the Greater London Council otherwise directs) a copy of a planning decision issued by a London Borough should be sent to the Greater London Council for their information.

The general rule, however, is subject to some exceptions.

Thus a statutory instrument may prescribe some classes of development, or development in some areas of Greater London, which will be dealt with by the Greater London Council, although, under the general provisions they belong to the jurisdiction of the London Boroughs. This exclusion, however, does not apply to the issue of an established use certificate.

On the other hand, the Greater London Council may, in a

particular case, although it would normally belong to its jurisdiction, entrust the London Borough with the carrying out of the enforcement procedure, including compensation for loss due to the issue of a stop notice.

The Greater London Council may, with the consent of the Secretary of State, delegate to the council of a London Borough any of those functions which are within the jurisdiction of the Greater London Council, and these functions will be performed by the London Borough council on behalf of the Greater London Council.

PART II

Compulsory Purchase and Compensation

Chapter 17

INTRODUCTION

The compulsory acquisition of land for public purposes is necessary in modern society. In many countries the government has the power to confiscate land for various purposes with, or without, compensation. However, in the United Kingdom compulsory acquisition can only be carried out if there is a power of acquisition granted by law, and the law invariably provides for compensation, which does not depend on the discretion of the acquiring authority, but must be effected according to existing legal provisions.

If land is compulsorily acquired — for whatever purpose — the following four stages have to be considered:

(a) there must be an Act of Parliament authorising the acquiring authority to purchase land compulsorily;

(b) the acquiring authority having the power to acquire land, has to select the land which it intends to purchase and has to obtain power to acquire that piece of land;

(c) when the acquiring authority has obtained power to purchase the selected land compulsorily, it must exercise this power and obtain ownership by the prescribed procedure;

(d) compensation should be assessed and paid by the acquiring authority.

After considering the historical background of the compulsory purchase law, the four stages described above will be dealt with.

Chapter 18

HISTORICAL BACKGROUND

It was in the closing years of the eighteenth and the first half of the nineteenth century, that, for the first time, powers for the compulsory purchase of land were given on a large scale to commercial undertakings such as canal and railway companies. Those undertakings, while sanctioned by the Parliament in the interests of the community, were primarily intended to be sources of profit to their promoters.

During those times the recognised method of obtaining compulsory purchase powers was by means of a Private Bill which might be opposed by interested parties during its Committee stage in either House before it became a Private Act.

Each Private Act prescribed its own procedure for the whole process of compulsory acquisition of land. Although these provisions were naturally similar in most cases, they could nonetheless be contested on each occasion by the opponents and the result was much unnecessary expense and a great waste of Parliament's time. For this reason the Land Clauses Consolidation Act 1845 was passed, which provided a remedy by incorporating in one Act the type of provisions formerly inserted in each separate Act, thus giving a complete code of law covering all questions pertaining to the exercise of the power, once it was granted by the Private Act. The provisions covered 'Notice to Treat', assessment and payment of compensation, right of entry on the land acquired, etc. This Act dealt not only with a host of provisions covering the problem of purchase itself, but also with the principles of compensations. Its purpose was, in the words of the preamble 'to consolidate in one Act certain provisions usually inserted in the Acts authorising the taking of land for undertakings of a public nature'.

In the middle of the nineteenth century the urgent sanitary problems resulting from the rapid urban expansion due to the Industrial Revolution necessitated the compulsory purchase of land y public authorities for numerous public health purposes, both under individual Town Improvement Acts and later under the Public Health Act 1875. From that time onwards powers of compulsory purchase were being given for many other purposes as for instance slum clearance, building of schools, new towns, atomic energy stations, etc.

As a consequence of these developments, the acquiring bodies are at present: government departments, local authorities and public corporations (British Railways, National Coal Board, British Broadcasting Corporation, etc.).

The procedure of Private Acts of Parliament was not appropriate for the host of compulsory purchases effected to-day and the powers of compulsory purchase are now given in general terms to the certain classes of public bodies, e.g. to local authorities for public health, housing or planning, under general Acts applying to the whole country.

Therefore the first stage of the procedure — the authorisation of compulsory purchase — is of secondary importance for the vast majority of cases, as general Acts, and particularly the Town and Country Planning Act 1971, grant the power in extremely wide terms (*see* Chapter 10).

The second stage of the procedure — the selection of land to be compulsorily acquired and the obtaining of power of acquisition in respect of this land, was, and still usually is, exercised by the acquiring body making an Order (after the general or private Act allows it) — a 'Compulsory Purchase Order' applying the compulsory purchase power conferred by the Act to the particular piece of land. The Order usually requires confirmation by an appropriate government department.

At one time each public general Act prescribed its own procedure for the making and confirmation of the Compulsory Purchase Order. Now uniformity of procedure has been achieved under the Acquisition of Land (Authorisation Procedure) Act 1946.

In some cases, however, this Act[1] requires that the Compulsory Purchase Order should be subject to the Special Parliamentary Procedure.[2] This means that such an order shall be of no effect, until laid before the Parliament in accordance with the provisions of the 1945 and 1965 Acts. Generally speaking, it means that Parliament may annul the order by a resolution of either House.

The following types of acquisition are subject to the Special

Parliamentary Procedure:

(a) land held by local authorities, statutory undertakers or the National Trust;

(b) Commons, open spaces and fuel and garden allotments;

(c) ancient monuments or other objects of archaeologica interest.

The third stage of the procedure — acquisition itself — originally governed by the Land Clauses Consolidation Act 1845, has now been replaced, with some amendments, by the Compulsory Purchase Act 1965. The provisions of this Act are substantially the same as those of the 1845 Act, which still has application to some compulsory purchases carried out under some older Acts.

The fourth stage is payment of compensation. Here again the Land Clauses Consolidation Act 1845 was replaced by the Acquisition of Land (Assessment of Compensation) Act 1919, which was afterwards repealed and replaced by the following two Acts:

(a) the Lands Tribunal Act 1949, which created a Tribunal with a wide jurisdiction covering amongst other things the problem of assessment of compensation whenever a dispute arises concerning the amount of compensation for the land acquired;

(b) the Land Compensation Act 1961, which is the present legal basis for the assessment of compensation.

Thus, as present, the law pertaining to compulsory purchase may be summarised as follows:

(a) there must be an Act of Parliament granting the powers to purchase land compulsorily for stated purpose (e.g. Town and Country Planning Act 1971 grants extensive powers to local authorities and Government Departments);

(b) these powers (in the vast majority of cases, with some insignificant exceptions) are obtained in respect of individual pieces of land under the Acquisition of Land (Authorisation Procedure) Act 1946;

(c) once the powers have been obtained they are usually exercised under the Compulsory Purchase Act 1965 (with a few exceptions, where the Land Clauses Consolidation Act 1845 still applies);

(d) the problem of compensation is dealt with under the Land Compensation Act 1961.

Chapter 19

OBTAINING OF COMPULSORY PURCHASE POWERS

In the vast majority of cases the procedure of obtaining compulsory powers in respect of a particular piece of land is governed by the Acquisition of Land (Authorisation Procedure) Act 1946. This Act covers almost all compulsory purchase with the following more important exceptions:

(a) purchases for the purpose of the New Town Act 1965[1]

(b) purchases under Part III of the Housing Act 1957 (Clearance Areas).[2]

The normal procedure under the 1946 Act may be summarised as follows:

The acquiring authority prepares a Compulsory Purchase Order for submission to the 'confirming authority'. This Order must identify the land to which the Order applies by a map. Before submitting the Order to the confirming authority the acquiring authority must publish a notice about the Order for two consecutive weeks in at least one local newspaper. This notice must confirm with the Regulations[3] and must state that the draft Order may be inspected and that objections may be made within a specified period being not less than 28 days. In addition a notice must be served on every owner, lessee and occupier of the land affected, except tenants for a month or less. If the acquiring authority cannot serve the notice on some persons (e.g. if the address is unknown), the confirming authority may allow the notice to be affixed to a conspicuous object on the land. Where the land is an ecclesiastical property (owned by the Church of England) notice must be served on the Church Commissioners.

If no objections are raised, or if all are withdrawn, the confirming authority, if satisfied that the proper notices have been published and served, may confirm the Order with, or without modification, but the area of land cannot be increased without the consent of all interested parties. If objections are made, the confirming authority must either hold an inquiry or, at least, give the objectors an opportunity of being heard by a person nominated by the confirming authority. The objector may be asked to state the grounds of his objections in writing and the confirming authority may ignore the objections, if they appear to relate exclusively to matters which can be dealt with by the Tribunal which assesses the compensation. Otherwise objections are not restricted to the legal matters; problems of policy, suitability of land for the intended purposes and other reasons may be raised by the objectors.

After considering the report of the Inspector who held the local inquiry or private hearing, the confirming authority (in most cases the Secretary of State for the Environment) may confirm the Order with, or without, modifications, or may refuse to confirm. The Secretary of State may be required to furnish reasons for his decision, but he may refuse to do so on grounds of national security. Confirmation of the Order must be advertised in the form prescribed by the Regulations and notice must be served on those persons who were notified previously on the preparation of the draft Order. The notice describes the land affected by the Order and indicates where the Order may be inspected.

A compulsory Purchase Order becomes operative from the date when notice of its confirmation is first published. Any person aggrieved may challenge its validity by an application to the High Court within six weeks of that date, on the grounds either:

(a) that the Order is *ultra vires* the Act; or

(b) that some essential requirements of the Act or of the Regulations made under it have not been complied with, and that in consequence his interests have been substantially prejudiced.

Unless the application is made to the Court within the prescribed period of six weeks, the Order cannot be questioned in any subsequent legal proceedings, not even if the Order was made in bad faith (Smith v. East Elloe Rural District Council 1956 A.C. 1 All E.R. 855).

Chapter 20

ACQUISITION OF LAND. PRELIMINARY PROBLEMS

Definition of Land in this Branch of Law

Both the Land Clauses Consolidation Act 1845 and the Compulsory Purchase Act 1965 define land in such a manner that it includes fixtures (e.g. buildings), rents, commons and profits *à prendre*. It also includes future real property rights, for instance options.

With regard to easements, it has been held by the Court that an owner cannot be compelled to grant easement over his land, unless the authorising Act clearly so provides.[1] He may grant it voluntarily or, if an easement is required by the acquiring authority, it has to purchase the land, which it would like to burden with an easement, compulsorily (Pinchin v. London and Blackwall Rail Co. 1954 3.W.R.52).

On the other hand, however, if the acquired land is a dominant tenement, then the easement is included in the purchase.

If the acquired land is a servient tenement, the easement over the land compulsorily acquired is not extinguished, but if the acquiring authority consequently interferes with the existing easement, then full compensation must be paid for the damage caused to the dominant tenement.

The Purpose for which Land May be Acquired

The purpose for which the land can be acquired is defined in the special or general Act granting the power to acquire land. If the land is acquired for other, secondary purposes, this may be allowed if these purposes are closely connected with the main purpose (e.g. purchase of land for railway purposes includes sidings and even car parks at the stations, but not a sand pit to extract the sand required for building the track (Galloway v. City of London 1866 13.W.R.701)).

Acquisition of Part of the Property

It often happens that only a part of a property is required by the acquiring authority. In this case the taking of a part may so alter the character of the remainder, as to make it of very little value to the owner.

Section 92 of the Land Clauses Consolidation Act 1845 gave some protection; this has been replaced by Section 8(1) of the Compulsory Purchase Act 1965, which provides that no person shall be required to sell a part of any 'house, building or manufactory' if it cannot be taken without material detriment to the land. In the case of a park or garden it is sufficient that taking a part would affect the amenity or convenience of the house. Disputes are determined by the Land Tribunal; if the Land Tribunal determines that the part of the land may be acquired, then it shall award compensation in respect of any loss due to the severance of the part proposed to be acquired, in addition to the value of the land. This additional compensation is called the compensation for 'injurious affection' and will be dealt with later (see Chapter 23).

Mines and Minerals under the Land Acquired

Where the land is acquired compulsorily, any coal mine in the land is excluded from the sale, with the obvious exception of any coal which it is necessary to dig out in the course of the operations for which land was acquired. All other minerals (except gold and silver which are Crown property under Common Law) would be included in the conveyance and have to be the subject of compensation by the acquiring authority.

The Railway Clauses Consolidation Act 1845 in Section 77-85 introduced provisions, whereby the acquiring authority may be relieved of this additional burden of compensation and the owner may be free to continue to work his minerals.

These provisions — known as the 'mining code' — are now of general application if incorporated in the Compulsory Purchase Order.

The main provisions of the mining code are:

(a) the acquiring authority will not be entitled to any mines of ironstone, slate or other materials;

(b) the authority may purchase them if they wish;

(c) if not purchased they can be worked by the owner (after giving 30 days' notice to the authority). There is the possibility of a counter notice, in which case compensation will be paid;

(d) even later the acquiring authority is entitled to serve a notice stopping work carried out by the previous owner. But if notice is not served, the owner is entitled to carry on with the extraction of the minerals.

Purchase of Land by Agreement

In many cases, in practice, land is acquired for statutory purposes by agreement between the parties and if so, the acquiring authority does not resort to compulsory powers. In such cases conveyance is effected in the same way as between private persons.

Alternative Procedures of Acquisition

The acquiring authority must exercise its power within three years after the Compulsory Purchase Order becomes operative, unless a special Act gives more time.

The usual procedure is to serve on the owners 'Notice to Treat', but in some cases it may be dispensed with by a 'General Vesting Declaration'.

Chapter 21

ACQUISITION OF LAND. PROCEDURE

Notice to Treat Procedure

The Notice to Treat is the notification of the acquiring authority's intention to purchase the owner's interest in a particular piece of land and of its willingness to pay compensation in respect of the loss arising from that acquisition.

The Notice to Treat should be served on all persons interested in, or having a power to sell and convey or release the land, so far as they are known to the acquiring authority after making diligent inquiries.

It must be served on the owners of the fee simple, leaseholders (with the important exception of tenants having no greater interest than for a year, or from year to year. Statutory tenants protected under the 1968 Rent Act belong to this category), mortgagees, but not owners of restrictive covenants or easements over the land, as these are not appropriated.

The exact form and wording of the Notice is immaterial, but Section 5(2) of the Compulsory Purchase Act 1965, provides that the Notice shall:

(a) give particulars of the land to which the Notice relates;

(b) demand particulars of the owner's interest and of his claim;

(c) state that the acquiring authority is willing to treat for the purchase of the land and for the compensation to be paid for damage due to execution of the works.

(In order that the details of the owner's interest may be obtained in a concise form, it is usual for the acquiring authority to enclose a special form of claim with the Notice to Treat, showing clearly the particulars required by the acquiring authority).

The legal consequences which follow the service of a valid Notice to Treat are:

(a) the owner may be forced to sell and the authority may be forced to purchase the land in question. Only in special

110

circumstances, explained below, may the Notice to Treat be withdrawn. If no agreement is reached as to the compensation, either party can ask for an assessment by the Lands Tribunal. The assessment of compensation, together with the Notice to Treat will then constitute a binding and enforceable contract, which may be the subject of specific performance by the Court;

(b) The Notice to Treat fixes the nature of the interest to be acquired. It is neither a contract for sale, nor a step putting in force the compulsory power. It is a neutral Act[1] which may be followed either by an agreement as to the price, or by an assessment of the compensation by the Lands Tribunal. Any changes of interest effected by the owner after the Notice to Treat do not affect the acquiring authority.

Until a few years ago, the Notice to Treat also fixed the amount of compensation. Since, however, the case of West Midland Baptist Trust) Association v. Birmingham Corporation (1969 3 All E.R. 172, 1970 A.C. 874, H.L. 3 W.L.R. 389), this is not so. This important case and its implications will be discussed later, when the amount of compensation will be dealt with.

As a general rule a Notice to Treat once issued cannot be withdrawn by the acquiring authority without the consent of the owner, except in the following circumstances:

(a) if the Notice to Treat refers to the part of the land belonging to the owner and he insists on selling the whole (Section 8(1) of the Compulsory Purchase Act 1965);

(b) it may be withdrawn within six weeks after the serving of the claim by the owner (Section 31(1) of the Land Compensation Act 1961);

(c) if a statement of claim is not delivered and the Lands Tribunal assesses the compensation, the authority may withdraw the Notice within six weeks (Section 31(2) of the Land Compensation Act 1961).

In all these cases it appears that the acquiring authority may withdraw after learning for the first time that the price is too high.

In the first two cases the acquiring authority has to pay compensation for any loss or expenses resulting from the issue and withdrawal of the Notice.

If both parties fail to act after the Notice to Treat has been issued, the result is that the Notice to Treat may become ineffective. The principles dealing with this situation were judicially enunciated in the leading case, Simpson Motor Sales London Ltd. v. Hendon Corporation (1963 2 All.E.R.484):

(a) it is the duty of the acquiring authority to proceed within a reasonable time;

(b) the acquiring authority may display an intention to abandon the purchase; delay in action may be an evidence of this;

(c) the Notice to Treat may be illegal and therefore not proceeded with;

(d) if there is inequitable conduct on the side of either party the Court may refuse to grant specific performance.

Although usually the acquiring authority obtains possession of the land in question after compensation has been assessed and paid, Section 11 of the Compulsory Purchase Act 1965 allows the acquiring authority to obtain possession earlier. Provided that the Notice to Treat has been served and a 14 days' notice has been given to all interested parties, the acquiring authority may enter upon the land. Compensation, which is either agreed between the parties or assessed by the Lands Tribunal will be paid with interest from the date of entry.

General Vesting Declaration Procedure

In addition to the usual procedure of acquiring land by using Notice to Treat procedure, recent legislation has introduced another procedure, which enables the acquiring authority to obtain ownership and possession of the land much more quickly than under the Notice to Treat procedure.

Section 30 of the Town and Country Planning Act 1968 (not repealed by the consolidating Act 1971) and Schedule 3 and 3A to the 1968 Act are the statutory basis for the 'General Vesting Declaration' procedure.

The more salient points of this procedure may be summarised as follows. If the acquiring authority decides to use this procedure they have to include a notice about it in the notification sent to the owners, etc. of the confirmation of the Compulsory Purchase Order. This notice may also be sent separately at a later date, but it may be sent only if no Notice to Treat has been issued.

The notice sent to the owners specifies the earliest date at which the General Vesting Declaration can be executed, which cannot be earlier than in two months time. The notice is registered in the local land charges register.

112

After the General Vesting Declaration has been executed, the acquiring authority has to serve on all interested persons (with the exception of occupiers holding under 'minor tenancies' or under 'tenancies about to expire') a notice in the prescribed form specifying the land and stating the effect of the declaration. The Vesting Declaration will take effect at the date stated which cannot be earlier than 28 days from the serving of the notice described in this paragraph.

As from the date on which the General Vesting Declaration takes effect the land specified will vest in the acquiring authority, which is entitled to take possession.

Tenants under minor tenancies or tenancies about to expire are entitled to 14 days' notice before possession is taken.

Compensation is either agreed between the parties or assessed by the Lands Tribunal, and is paid with the interest since the Vesting Declaration date.

Schedules 3 and 3A contain detailed provisions in respect of the possibilities of withdrawal of the General Vesting Declaration. Generally speaking, once the General Vesting Declaration has been executed it has similar legal effects as if a Notice to Treat has been served and the possibilities of withdrawing the General Vesting Declaration are similar to the possibilities of withdrawing of the Notice to Treat, but the acquiring authority cannot withdraw the General Vesting Declaration solely because the assessment of compensation is higher than was anticipated. They can do so, however, if the owner objects to the severance of his property and his claim is sustained by the Lands Tribunal.

Chapter 22

COMPENSATION. HISTORICAL BACKGROUND

When an owner is deprived of his interest in land under statutory powers, he is entitled to compensation for the loss of that interest as a matter of right, unless Parliament expressly deprives him of that right (Attorney General v. De Keysers Royal Hotel Ltd.).[1]

The Town and Country Planning Acts and particularly the Acts enacted since 1947 created difficulty in assessment of compensation, as each piece of land may be considered as having a dual value. Firstly 'the existing use value', which is the value of the land in its present use, and secondly the 'market value' which is very often considerably higher if planning permission is either already granted, or where there is every expectation that it would be granted.

The measure of compensation for land compulsorily acquired has been affected by the provisions of the following Acts, which together cover the period of over 120 years:

The Land Clauses Consolidation Act 1845.

Until 1 January 1966 this Act was incorporated into every Act which gave compulsory powers, except in so far as its provisions were expressly modified or excluded.

The compensation provisions of the Act were peculiarly vague. But certain basic principles were established in the course of their interpretation by the Courts and may be summarised as follows:

(a) compensation for the land should include compensation for disturbance and other loss suffered by the owner in consequence of its acquisition;

(b) service of Notice to Treat determines the property, the nature of the interest taken and determines the date of valuation. This last principle has been abandoned recently in the case of West Midland Baptist (Trust) Association v. Birmingham Corporation (*see* page 117);

(c) the burden of compensation cannot be increased after Notice o Treat (e.g. the right to extend a legal lease by the lessee is to be taken into account, but not the possibility of renewal, even if this renewal was granted after the Notice to Treat had been issued);

d) the value to be assessed is the value to the owner and not to the acquiring authority.

The Acquisition of Land (Assessment of Compensation) Act 1919

This Act prescribes that the general basis of compensation should be the price of land which may be expected to be realised if sold in the open market by a willing seller. This price is known as the 'open market value' and it includes the development value which the land possesses.

The Town and Country Planning Act 1944

Under this Act, issued as a temporary measure for the duration of the war, the open market value during the period from 17 November 1944 to 6 August 1947 was assessed for compensation purposes by reference to the prices prevailing at 31 March 1939. Thus war and post-war inflation was to be disregarded.

The Town and Country Planning Acts 1947 and 1954

These Acts applied to compensation payable under Notices to Treat served between 6 August 1947 and 30 October 1958. The general basis of compensation under these Acts was 'existing use value', assessed on the assumption that planning permission would be given only for the very limited forms of development specified in the Third Schedule to the Town and Country Planning Act 1947 (these are so called 'existing use developments', now given in the Schedule 8 to the 1971 Town and Country Planning Act and were described in Chapter 13).

The Town and Country Planning Act 1959

This Act restored 'open market value' as a general principle but with certain prescribed 'assumptions' in respect of planning permission, which considerably lowered the full market value.

The Land Compensation Act 1961

As from 1 August 1961 this Act applies to all cases where land is authorised to be acquired compulsorily. It re-enacts the general principles of the 1919 Act and the principal compensation provisions of the Town and Country Planning Act 1959.

Chapter 23

COMPENSATION UNDER THE LAND COMPENSATION ACT 1961

Compensation for the Land Acquired

The Act does not affect the owner's general right to compensation under the 1845 and 1965 Acts, but it contains some important modifications in the principles governing assessment.

Section 5 of the Act lays down six rules for assessing compensation in respect of land acquired. Five of these rules concern the value of the land itself; the sixth rule affirms the right of the owner to obtain further compensation, not connected with the value of the land, as for injurious affection and disturbance.

Rule 1

'No allowance shall be made on account of the acquisition being compulsory.'

When the value of the land was assessed under the Land Clauses Consolidation Act 1845, it became customary for the referees assessing the value to add 10% of the value of the land as additional compensation for the forced sale. This custom has now been expressly excluded.

Rule 2

'The value of land shall, subject as hereinafter provided, be taken to be the amount which the land, if sold in the open market by a willing seller, might be expected to realise.'

Thus this Rule accepts the principle of 'open market value'. The fact, however, that all land is now under strict planning control gives 'open market value' a special meaning, different from the meaning in 1919 when it was first clearly formulated. For, in the land capable of further development, 'the amount which the land ... might be expected to realise', will depend on the kind of development for which, having regard to the current

116

development plan for the area, planning permission is likely to be obtained.

The Act, therefore, provides for certain assumptions as to the grant of planning permission to be made, and these assumptions will be discussed later.

There is another important factor on which the value of the land would depend, namely the date by reference to which the price is to be fixed. In the nineteenth century when prices were relatively static, this problem was of no importance and the date of issue of the Notice to Treat had been accepted as the convenient date governing the assessment of price. Nowadays, however, if some years elapse between the issue of the Notice to Treat and payment of compensation, the owner may be detrimentally affected by being paid the price prevailing some years ago. This problem came before the Court recently and although it concerned the assessment under Rule 5 ('equivalent reinstatement'), the House of Lords *obiter* states that the same rule should apply to the assessment of the price of land under Rule 2. The facts of the case (West Midland Baptist (Trust) Association v. Birmingham Corporation (H.L.) 1969, 3 All E.R. 172) are as follows:

Birmingham Corporation in carrying out a large improvement scheme in the centre of the City, acquired a Baptist Chapel compulsorily. The Notice to Treat was deemed to have been served on 14 August 1947 (its legality was not questioned), but the property was vested in the Birmingham Corporation only in 1963. The point at issue was the date by reference to which the amount of compensation was to be fixed and it was agreed that compensation should be assessed on the basis of equivalent reinstatement. If the relevant date was the date of the Notice to Treat (1947) the compensation would amount to £50,000; if the appropriate date would be the date when reinstatement might reasonably begin (1961) then the compensation would amount to some £90,000. The House of Lords unanimously decided that the latter date should govern the assessment. Their Lordships stated that although in the nineteenth century the date was immaterial, as prices were static, and the date of Notice to Treat was a convenient date, nowadays, due to inflation it is essential that the date must be as late as reasonable. Thus, in future, the date of taking possession by the acquiring authority, or the date of assessment of compensation, whichever is the earlier, should govern the amount of compensation.

117

Rule 3

'The special suitability or adaptability of the land for any purpose shall not be taken into account, if that purpose is a purpose to which it could be applied only in pursuance of statutory powers, or for which there is no market apart from the needs of a particular purchaser or the requirements of any authority possessing compulsory powers.'

This is simply an expression of the principle contained in the Land Clauses Consolidation Act 1845 that the value to be assessed is the value to the owner and not to the acquiring authority. The authority may require badly a piece of land of negligible value for a specific purpose (say, for an atomic reactor). Only this negligible value will be taken into account, as the project can be realised only 'in pursuance of statutory powers'.

Rule 4

'Where the value of the land is increased by reason of the use thereof or of any premises thereon in a manner which could be restrained by the Court, or is contrary to law, or is detrimental to the health of the inmates or to the public health, the amount of that increase shall not be taken into account.'

This rule is self-explanatory.

Rule 5

'Where the land is, and but for the compulsory acquisition would continue to be, devoted to a purpose of such a nature, that there is no general demand or market for land for that purpose, the compensation may, if the Lands Tribunal is satisfied that reinstatement in some other place is bona fide intended, be assessed on the basis of the reasonable cost of equivalent reinstatement.'

This rule applies to such buildings as chapels, schools, almhouses and similar institutions.

Rule 6

'The provision of Rule 2 shall not affect the assessment of compensation for disturbance or other matter not directly based on the valuation of land.'

The whole matter of compensation for disturbance and injurious affection will be dealt with later in this Chapter.

Sections 6, 7 and 8 of the Land Compensation Act contain

additional rules for the assessment of compensations:

(a) 'No account should be taken of any increase or decrease in value due to the development under the acquiring body scheme.'

The reason for this rule is that the development of the acquiring body is of such a large or special scale (e.g. a new town) that they would not be carried out if the land would not be compulsorily acquired. This principle was formulated by Lord MacDermott in a Privy Council case,[1] when he said that the increase of the value of the land will be disregarded, if it is 'entirely due to the scheme underlying the acquisition'.

(b) any increase in the value of adjacent or contiguous land of the same owner shall be set off against the compensation payable for land taken from him. In subsequent acquisition of this 'adjacent land' the amount overpaid or underpaid will be set off.

Any decrease in the value of land belonging to the same person is compensated under the heading 'injurious affection'.

(c) the loss of value due to the threat of compulsory acquisition should be ignored.

Although it is simple enough to say (as Rule 2 does) that: 'compensation for acquisition of land by public authorities will be the price which the property would obtain in the open market', a problem arises, as the value of property cannot be considered without regard to planning permission, already granted or obtainable. This problem is solved by Section 14-22 of the Compulsory Purchase Act 1961.

Three sets of rules can be discerned:

(a) Section 15 requires some general assumptions regarding planning permission to be accepted in assessing the compensation:

(i) where the authority's proposals involve the development of the land to be acquired, it shall be assumed that planning permission would be given to this development;

(ii) it shall be assumed that planning permission would be given for any form of development specified in the Third Schedule of the Town and Country Planning Act 1962 ('existing use developments' now contained in the Schedule 8 of the 1971 Act);

(iii) it shall be assumed that planning permission would be granted for development of any class specified in a 'certificate for appropriate development' issued under Sections 17-22 of the Land Compensation Act 1961;

119

(iv) if there is a development plan the assumption is that the planning permission would be granted in accordance with the development plan in existence.

Points (iii) and (iv) require some explanation.

Where an interest in land is proposed to be acquired and that land does not consist of an area defined in the development plan as an area of comprehensive development, or allocated for residential, commercial or industrial purposes, it may be difficult to decide what planning assumptions are appropriate. In such situations either party may apply to the local planning authority for a certificate stating what development might reasonably have been expected to be permitted if the land had not been subject to compulsory purchase. When such a certificate is issued, planning permission for such development will be assumed in assessing the value of the land. Against refusal of the certificate or if the certificate is not satisfactory, the party may appeal to the Secretary of State, with a further appeal (on limited grounds) to the High Court. A Statutory Instrument (Land Compensation Development Order 1963 S.I.749) contains detailed provisions in respect of the issue of the certificate and appeals.

In a case where there is a development plan there may still be some problems as to how to apply its provisions to the possibilities of development of the land being acquired. Section 16 of the Land Compensation Act 1961 contains detailed assumptions as to how the development plan's provisions should be applied to the land in question.

Compensation for Disturbance

Where the land is compulsorily acquired, the owner is entitled to compensation not only for the value of the interest in the land, but also for the loss he has suffered from being disturbed in the enjoyment of it. This principle is recognised by the Rule 6 of the Section 5 of the Land Compensation Act 1961 and was also pronounced clearly in the leading case (Horn v. Sunderland Corporation 1941 1 All E.R. 480), when Scott J. said: 'the owner has the right to receive money payment not less than the loss imposed on him in the public interest, but on the other hand no greater'.

Although the principle is clear, the precise operation is not easy to ascertain, but from the numerous cases decided it appears that the following losses have been recognised:

120

(a) the cost of removal with incidental expenses (e.g. alteration of curtains and carpets), but not the higher rent paid in the new place, as it is assumed that the higher rent is due to the better premises;

(b) incidental expenses, e.g. the notification of change of address, the transfer of the telephone, etc;

(c) depreciation of fixtures due to removal;

(d) depreciation of stock;

(e) diminution of value of goodwill if any;

(f) the cost of the surveyor who examined the new premises, even if he advised against buying them and the transaction did not materialise.

Injurious affection

Compensation for injurious affection may be defined as compensation for owners whose land is injuriously affected by the undertaking for which compulsory purchase has been effected.

In this connection two types of claim should be separately considered:

(a) claims where land affected is held by the same person with the land taken;

(b) claims where the land affected is not held with the land taken.

With regard to the first category, it must be shown that the land was held with the land acquired, although it is not required that it should be contiguous. The test is, whether the possession of both pieces enhances the value as the whole.

The compensation is due under two headings: loss of the value due to severance of a part of the land and injurious affection as such (due to dust, smell, noise, loss of privacy, etc).

The measure of damage is the depreciation of value of the land.

Under the second category claims where the land affected is not held with the land taken are dealt with by Section 10 of the Compulsory Purchase Act 1965. Here the possibility of obtaining compensation is very limited.[2]

Compensation is given as a substitute for damages which may be due for any tort which would be committed by the acquiring authority, but for its defence of acting under the statutory authority. This means that it is only due if damages would be recoverable under the law of tort. It is due only if there is a physical interference with any right, easement or natural right of fee simple owner. There are the following conditions for claiming compensation:

(a) the injury must result from some act which was made lawful under the statutory powers granted to the acquiring authority;

(b) the injury must be such as it would be actionable but for the statutory powers;

(c) it must be an injury to land and not injury to the person or trade;

(d) it must flow from the execution of work and not from the subsequent use of the land acquired.

If land of a third person is increased in value due to execution of work, no payment may be required from the owner for this 'betterment'.

Compensation for Yearly Tenancies and Lesser Interests

Although these persons are not entitled to receive the notice to treat, they are entitled to some compensation under Section 20 of the Compulsory Purchase Act 1965. Their compensation is limited to the value of unexpired term and for any other injury or loss they may sustain. In the case of a tenancy of business premises the tenant is entitled to compensation assessed either under this heading or under the 1954 Landlord and Tenant Act (as amended by the 1969 Law Property Act), whichever is the greater.

Under the Land Compensation Act 1961, Section 10, the acquiring authority may pay such reasonable allowance as it thinks fit in respect of removal expenses, or loss by disturbance of trade or business to persons displaced from any house or other building. This Section covers cases where there is no legal duty to pay compensation, but where the acquiring authority considers that some payment should reasonably be made to persons displaced, and the Section gives the statutory powers to make these *ex gratia* payments.

Chapter 24

LANDS TRIBUNAL

Section 1 of the Land Compensation Act 1961 provides that in any case where the land is compulsorily acquired, any question of disputed compensation shall be referred to the Lands Tribunal and shall be determined by the Tribunal.

The Lands Tribunal, set up under the Land's Tribunal Act 1949, exercises its jurisdiction not only in respect of compensation for land compulsorily acquired, but also in many other cases where valuation of the land is involved. Section 1 of the Land Tribunal Act specifies the Tribunal's jurisdiction.

The Lands Tribunal consists of a   resident, who must be a person who held judicial office, or a barrister of at least seven years' standing, and of other members who are barristers, solicitors or valuers appointed after consultation with the President of the Royal Institute of Chartered Surveyors.

The jurisdiction of the Lands Tribunal may be exercised by any one or more members (this is decided by the President).

Under Section 3(4) of the Lands Tribunal Act 1949 a decision of the Lands Tribunal shall be final, but any person aggrieved by the decision may appeal by way of case stated to the Court of Appeal on a point of law.

Special procedural provisions have been enacted by the Land Compensation Act 1961 (Section 2) with respect to any proceedings before the Tribunal dealing with compensation for land compulsorily acquired.

Under these provisions:

(a) the Lands Tribunal shall sit in public;

(b) generally no more than one expert witness on either side shall be heard;

(c) a member of the Lands Tribunal shall be entitled to enter on and inspect any land which is subject to the proceedings;

(d) the Lands Tribunal shall, on the application of either party,

123

specify the amount awarded in respect of any particular matter the subject of the award.

The detailed provisions covering procedure at the Lands Tribunal are contained in the Lands Tribunal Rules.[1]

Proceedings start by a notice of reference on a prescribed form and in the manner stated in Rule 16. A copy of the Notice to Treat and the Notice of Claim must accompany the notice of reference.

The procedure before the Tribunal is prescribed in Parts VII and VIII of the Rules; the main provisions may be summarised as follows:

The Tribunal has power to make an order for discovery of documents, particulars and interrogatories. Notice must be given if a valuer is to be called; the expert witness's valuation must be sent to the Tribunal.

The proceedings are opened by the party claiming compensation. Evidence is usually given orally, but with the consent of the parties or by the direction of the Tribunal affidavits are allowed. Witnesses make their depositions under oath. Any party may appear and be heard either in person, or by counsel or solicitor, or by any other person allowed by leave of the Tribunal to appear instead of the party.

A party may ask for a preliminary hearing on a point of law. If the Tribunal so decides, it may give an alternative finding as the amount which it would have awarded, if it had decided the point of law differently.

The acquiring authority may make an unconditional offer of compensation; if it is accepted, it will constitute a binding contract for sale. If such an unconditional offer is not accepted and the question of compensation is referred to the Tribunal, the amount of the offer must not be disclosed to the Tribunal until the compensation has been decided, but a copy of the offer may be sent to the Registrar and shall be opened by the Tribunal after the decision about the amount of compensation has been made. Under Section 4 of the Land Compensation Act 1961 if the Lands Tribunal award does not exceed the offer, the Tribunal (if there are no exceptional circumstances) shall order the claimant to bear the costs.

124

==

NOTES

==

Chapter 1
1 Town and Country Planning (Amendment) Act 1951
  Town and Country Planning Act 1953
  Town and Country Planning Act 1954
  Town and Country Planning Act 1959
2 Cmnd 3333
3 Chapter 70

Chapter 2
1 Section 224(1)(d)
2 A. E. Telling — Planning Law and Procedure Chapter 3
3 General Development Order 1963 (No 709) as amended in 1969
  (No 276)
4 Chapter 12
5 Section 1 of the Local Government Act 1972 and Schedule 1
6 Schedule 4 of the Local Government Act 1972
7 Section 1(1) and (2) of the Town and Country Planning Act 1971
  as amended by the Local Government Act 1972. Thus this
  organisation of the local planning authorities will come into
  existence on 1 April 1974

Chapter 3
1 Town and Country Planning (Development Plans) Regulations
  1965 No 1453
2 Errington v. Minister of Housing and Local Government (1935)
  32 L.G.R.481
3 Town and Country Planning Act 1968 (Commencement No 6)
  (Teesside etc) Order 1971 S.I. No 1109
  Town and Country Planning Act 1968 (Commencement No 7)
  (South Hampshire) Order 1971 S.I. No 2079
  Town and Country Planning Act 1968 (Commencement No 8)
  (Leicester-Leicestershire) Order 1971 S.I. No 2080
  Town and Country Planning Act 1971 (Commencement No 1)

(West Midland) Order 1972 S.I. 1060

Town and Country Planning Act 1971 (Commencement No 5 (West Midland) Order 1972 S.I. No 1364

Town and Country Planning Act 1971 (Commencement No 6 (Buckinghamshire) Order 1972 S.I. No 1408

Town and Country Planning Act 1971 (Commencement No 7 (South East Wales) Order 1972 S.I. No 1519

Town and Country Planning Act 1971 (Commencement No 8 (North Wales) Order 1972 S.I. No 1520

Town and Country Planning Act 1971 (Commencement No 9 (Brighton etc) Order 1972, S.I. No 1559

Town and Country Planning Act 1971 (Commencement No 10 (Norfolk and East Suffolk etc) Order 1972 S.I. No 2032

Chapter 4

1 Street v. Essex C.C. (1965) 193 Estate Gazette p.537
2 Scholes v. Min. H. and L.G. and Heysham B.C. (1966) 197 Estate Gazette p.563
3 McKeller v. Min. H. and L.G. (1966) Estate Gazette 6 May 1966
4 Belmont Farm Ltd v. Minister of Housing and Local Government and another (1962) 60. L.G.R. 319
5 Hidderley v. Warwickshire County Council (1963) 61. L.G.R. 266
6 Issued in 1963 S.I. 709, amended in 1954 (S.I. 1239), 1965 (S.I. 498), 1967 (S.I. 1076), 1968 (S.I. 1623) and in 1969 (S.I. 276). Reissued as consolidated Order in 1973 — Town and Country Planning General Development Order 1973 S.I.31 — see Appendix 'A'
7 Southend-on-Sea Corporation v. Hodgson (Wickford) Ltd. (1961) 2. W.L.R. 806

Chapter 6

1 See page 46.
2 Town and Country Planning (Tree Preservation Order) Regulations 1969 S.I. No 17
3 Town and Country Planning (Control of Advertisements) Regulations 1969 S.I. No 1532, as amended by the Town and Country Planning (Control of Advertisements) (Amendment) Regulations 1972 S.I. 482

Chapter 7
1 Schedule 16 to the Local Government Act 1972

Chapter 8
1 Sections 87-111

Chapter 10
1 A. E. Telling. Planning Law and Procedure 3rd Ed. page 163

Chapter 11
1 Report of the Committee on Compensation and Betterment ('Uthwatt Report') 1942 Cmnd 6386

Chapter 18
1 Part III of the First Schedule of the 1946 Act
2 Statutory Orders (Special Procedure) Acts 1945 and 1965

Chapter 19
1 Schedules 3 and 4 of the New Town Act 1965
2 Schedule 3 of the Housing Act 1957
3 Compulsory Purchase of Land Regulations 1949 S.I. No 507

Chapter 20
1 Section 113 of the Town and Country Planning Act 1971 so provides

Chapter 21
1 Holloway and another v. Dover Corporation (1960) 2 All E.R. 193

Chapter 22
1 (1920) A.C.508

Chapter 23
1 Pointe Gourde Quarrying and Transport Co v. Sub Intendent of Crown Lands (1947) A.C. 565
2 The new Land Compensation Bill received a second reading in the House of Commons on 27 November 1972 and has been referred to a Standing Committee for consideration.

The Bill, which consists of 66 clauses and two Schedules is

divided into six parts. The Bill supplements the existing law rather
than amends it and introduces only minor amendments to the
Land Compensation Act 1961 and the Compulsory Purchase Act
1965.

The most important provision is a new right of compensation
when the value of land has depreciated by physical factors caused
by public works, even if the land is not held together with the
land compulsorily acquired

Chapter 24
1 S.I. 1963 No 483

BIBLIOGRAPHY

Brown, Harold J. J., *Encyclopedia of the Law of Compulsory Purchase and Compensation*, Sweet and Maxwell

Davies, Keith, *Law of Compulsory Purchase and Compensation*, Butterworth

Hamilton, R. N. D., *A Guide to Development and Planning*, Fifth Edition, Oyez Publications

Heap, Desmond, Editor, *Encyclopedia of Planning*, Sweet and Maxwell

Heap, Desmond, *An Outline of Planning Law*, Fifth Edition, Sweet and Maxwell

Lawrence, David M. and Moore, Victor, *Compulsory Purchase and Compensation*, Fifth Edition, *The Estates Gazette*

Parrish, Harold, *Cripps on Compulsory Acquisition of Land, Powers, Procedure and Compensation*, Stevens and Sons

Telling, A. E., *Planning Law and Procedure*, Third Edition, Butterworth

Appendix A

NEW GENERAL DEVELOPMENT ORDER

On 1 March 1973 a new General Development Order under the Town and Country Planning Act 1971 came into effect. (The Town and Country Planning General Development Order 1973 S.I. No 31.) This Order consolidates the provisions of the 1963 Order and five subsequent amending orders and introduces a number of alterations, the most important being:

The 'bad neighbour developments' — Section 26 of the 1971 Act (page 45) — have been extended by adding the following developments: buildings over 20 metres in height, casinos, fun fairs, bingo halls, kennels, zoos, scrapyards, coalyards and cemeteries, also mineral workings, motor and motor-cycle sports and the killing and plucking of poultry.

Class I of 'permitted developments' (page 28) include three new types of development: porches of limited size, even if they extend beyond the front of the house and exceed the cubic content allowance, hardstanding for vehicles incidental to the enjoyment of the house and oil storage tanks for domestic heating, subject to certain limitations.

The 'standard conditions' (page 28) have been removed and replaced by a general limitation which now appears as article 3(3) of the Order.

Appendix B

LAND COMPENSATION BILL

This Bill, which received a second reading in the House of Commons on 27 November 1972, has been referred to a Standing Committee for consideration.

Part I deals with compensation for depreciation caused by public works. The public works are: any highway, aerodrome or works or and provided or used in the exercise of statutory powers. The factors giving a claim for compensation are noise, vibration, smell, fumes, smoke, artificial lighting and discharge of any solid or liquid substance. The basis for the claim has to arise on or after 17 October 1972. The Bill contains detailed provisions for the method of assessing the compensation; the general principle is that the compensation amounts to depreciation of value of the land caused by the use of any public works.

Part II authorises the Secretary of State to make regulations in respect of insulating buildings against noise caused by the construction or use of public works.

A highway authority may acquire by agreement any land affected in its enjoyment by the construction or use of the highway (which presumably means the land adjoining the highway). Similar powers are granted for the purpose of mitigating any adverse effect on the land adjoining other public works.

Part III creates a new heading of compensation 'home loss payment'. (It is renewal of the payment made under the Land Clauses Consolidation Act 1845, which has been expressly abolished by the Rule 1 of Section 5 of the Land Compensation Act 1961). The amount of compensation, if the date of displacement is before 1 April 1973, is an amount equivalent to the rateable values of the dwelling multiplied by seven, if the displacement takes place after that date, multiplied by three, but in neither case can it exceed £1,500.

The Bill creates also a 'farm loss payment' amounting to averag annual profit derived from the use of the farm, computed b reference to the last three years.

Persons without compensatable interests are entitled to dis turbance payments amounting to reasonable removal expenses, an for persons carrying on a trade or business the loss by reason of the disturbance of that trade or business.

Where a person is displaced from a dwelling and suitable accom modation is not available on reasonable terms, the particula authority must provide the person affected with other suitable accommodation.

Part IV of the Bill contains new provisions amending assessmen of compensation. Injurious affection is given a wider definition. It will be assessed by reference to the whole of the works and not only the part situated on the land acquired of the person affected. There is a right of persons entitled to compensation to ask, under certain conditions, for advance payment of compensation.

Part V of the Bill amends provisions in respect of planning blight (Sections 192 to 207 of the Town and Country Planning Act 1971) enlarging the classes of blighted land, but retaining the main principle that only the land threatened by the compulsory purchase may be considered to be blighted.

INDEX